EXPERIENTIAL LEARNING PACKAGES

The Instructional Design Library

Volume 23

EXPERIENTIAL LEARNING PACKAGES

Sivasailam Thiagarajan
Instructional Alternatives
Bloomington, Indiana

Danny G. Langdon
Series Editor

Educational Technology Publications
Englewood Cliffs, New Jersey 07632

ANGLE

Library of Congress Cataloging in Publication Data

Thiagarajan, Sivasailam.
    Experiential learning packages.

    (The Instructional design library; v. 23)
    Bibliography: p.
    1. Verbal learning. 2. Experience. I. Title.
II. Series: Instructional design library; v. 23.
LB1059.T45   370.15'2   79-23414
ISBN 0-87778-143-5

Printed in the United States of America.

Library of Congress Catalog Card Number:
79-23414.

International Standard Book Number:
0-87778-143-5.

First Printing: March, 1980.

FOREWORD

It is obviously a bit trite to say it, but reading this book is an experience. One could take that in several ways, but in my case—and, I am confident, in your own—it will all be positive.

While the entire "package" description in this book is worthy of careful attention, I was particularly delighted to find substantive guidelines on the "debriefing" aspect of the design. These guidelines are useful not only in relation to this design structure, but for many other designs as well. It has always troubled me to "debrief" an experience with students—particularly when the students are my peers. I have learned from this book how to do it better.

For the purist, there may be some question as to whether the Experiential Learning Package is a unique design in and of itself or really a collection of designs. This is supported in some small manner by the author's own admissions. However, one soon comes to appreciate it as being a unique design, upon careful inspection of the debriefing aspect in particular. Certainly, learning takes place through the experience segment itself—where we usually think it takes place—but this author gives us clear insight into where most of the learning *really* takes place: the debriefing segment. This should give us all a new or certainly heightened revelation of the importance of debriefing. How do I know? I *tried* it—and experience tells me so.

Danny G. Langdon
Series Editor

PREFACE

I have been using experiential learning techniques for many years in my training career without consciously thinking about their definition or design. I considered them to be minor devices in my training tool kit until a few years ago, when I met some stubborn friends. After initial instruction, they refused to learn from my inspiring lectures or effective materials but chose instead to do their own postgraduate "thing" on the firing line. During the past few years, I forgot to say, "I could have told you that" or "But that's exactly what I told you two years ago," as I watched in fascination how my friends gained competence and confidence by working through a set of experiences.

Suddenly, experiential learning acquired a significant saliency in my life. I became aware that I could package my techniques; I rationally reflected on the product and objectively analyzed the developmental process. I discovered the importance of debriefing and of balancing freedom and structure in learning. I also read extensively in this area. I did not agree with everything I read. I decided not to worry about the philosophy but to focus on practical procedures for developing a product which I define somewhat idiosyncratically. The prescriptions in this book come out of my analysis and reading; they have been verified and validated with individuals who came to dinner and with groups which attended my workshops and my friends' courses at Indiana University and at the University of Montreal.

I would like to dedicate this book to my special friend, Diane, for the role she played in shaping my approach to this instructional design format. With her stubbornness, she made me aware of the affective advantages of this approach. In addition, she has been a co-experiencer in a number of learning events all around the world. She has been a debriefer after many a joyful and traumatic experience, and above everything else, she has been a delightfully friendly experience.

S.T.

CONTENTS

ABSTRACT

EXPERIENTIAL LEARNING PACKAGES

There are two major types of learning: The first takes place in a classroom and deals with the dissemination of symbolized and codified knowledge. The second takes place in the real world through direct, meaningful experience and rational reflection on the contents and the consequences of this experience. This book is about instructional materials that use the structure of verbalized learning to increase the effectiveness of experiential learning.

An experiential learning package is an instructional material that specifies a relevant experience and provides a procedure of analyzing this experience to help the learners achieve a specific instructional goal. The package may come in different forms and sizes, and specify different activities for the learners and their leaders.

This instructional design format is especially suited for use with learners who have insufficient or excessive verbal fluency. Experiential learning packages help learners to effectively attain affective, empathic, interactive, and complex-cognitive objectives. They also help people unlearn undesirable prejudices and phobias. They are especially recommended for vocational education in the helping professions and in instructional situations that involve internships. Very simple or very abstract tasks are not suited for this format.

The components of an experiential package include materials for structuring the experience and organizing the debriefing. These materials may provide instructions and background information to the learners and their leaders. The experiential section may use different instructional designs. The debriefing section has two phases, the first for clearing the air and the second for exploring the experience and drawing inferences.

The systems-approach model to instructional development may be applied to the design and development of experiential learning packages with suitable modifications. This model consists of the stages of analysis and prescription, design and development, and verification and revision. Specific guidelines for various steps within each of these stages are provided in the book, as well as two alternative models for the design and development of experiential learning packages.

EXPERIENTIAL LEARNING PACKAGES

I.

USE

This book is not about experiential learning as an abstract educational construct. It is about the *experiential learning package,* which is a concrete training material and which is defined in an idiosyncratic manner. Depending on your choice of definition of "experiential learning" from the wide (and conflicting) variety currently available in the growing literature, you may dislike and disagree with the conceptual basis of the author, or you may find it a useful addition to your instructional-design tool kit.

There are two major types of learning available to us: The first type usually takes place in the classroom with the aid of lectures, textbooks, and examinations. This type of learning is heavily dependent upon the dissemination of symbolized, verbalized, and codified knowledge. This is the type of education with which we are most familiar. It is also the type we are best prepared to benefit from, both through formal education and through the media. We have considerable skills in processing printed and spoken information and in learning from it.

The second type of learning usually takes place in the street or in the workplace through direct experiences. While the cliché tells us that experience is the best teacher, there is no automatic guarantee that *all* experiences will provide useful learning. If this were so, we would all be smart and never make the same mistake twice. Also, older people would be significantly more wise than younger ones. But we know this is not true. Experience is an essential ingredient for learning, but it is not sufficient. What is required, in addition, is the act of reflecting upon the experience and deriving useful lessons from it.

There is room for both types of learning in our educational system, in training programs, and in lifestyles. Certain types of instructional objectives, learner groups, subject-matter areas, and educational situations appear to benefit more from the verbal approach than from the experiential one. However, other objectives, learners, and subject-matter areas lend themselves better to the experiential approach.

Experiential learning packages facilitate the second type of learning. In this instructional design format, a relevant experience is carefully selected or created. The learner is left to feel and work through this experience without any distracting didactics. Immediately following the experience, a debriefing session helps the learner to reflect upon this experience and discover useful concepts and competencies. By providing a retrospective structure to the experiential component, this debriefing attempts to combine the best of verbal learning with the nonverbal type.

The primary purpose of this chapter is to discuss the use of experiential learning packages. Rather than attempting such a discussion in abstract, let's begin with a few examples.

EXAMPLE 1: STUPID STUDENTS

Dr. Dormer was not sure if she wanted to try out that experiential learning package in her educational methods course, but she decided that there was no better method of illustrating the point she wanted to make. She could always terminate the activity if somebody really began to hurt. She also felt that during debriefing everything could be straightened up.

The package contained enough materials for five to 15 participants and she had no problem figuring out the exact requirements for her 12 students. She had to select one of them to be her accomplice to set up the experience. She used the random procedure recommended in the instructor's manual and ended up with Bill. She called Bill on the telephone and explained that they were doing a microteaching session the next day and he would be playing the role of the teacher. Everyone in her course had done microteaching earlier and all it involved was for one of them to be the teacher and the others to pretend to be elementary school students. But this time, there was a twist to the activity. Instead of a typical elementary school topic, the students were to learn a method for deciphering a secret code. Bill was given the basic training and the instructional objectives. He was also given certain secret instructions.

The session began smoothly the next day. The "teacher" explained the procedure for decoding secret messages. He showed how to guess the substituted letters based on frequency and other clues. Each "student" was given a dittoed worksheet, and the teacher wanted to see who could solve the cipher first. Susan was a little apprehensive, and she felt uncomfortable about the implied competition. Even before she could try out a couple of guesses and find out that they did not work, four or five hands went up excitedly. Susan felt stupid when the "teacher" went to these kids' desks and confirmed that they had successfully broken the code. After a couple of minutes, Bill announced that rather than hold back the smarter kids while the slower ones plodded along, he wanted all students to share the solution. Susan felt more stupid when she found out that everyone was working on the same cipher. She was hoping that different students had different ciphers and that those who had solved theirs earlier had easier ones. She felt really humiliated when Bill asked her if she had figured out at least a couple of words. The other kids started showing off and Susan remembered that she always hated puzzles, her GRE score was low on the verbal side, and she had problems with spelling. Some of the other kids were smugly reporting how easy the whole thing had been. Susan was happy to find that Don, another student in the course, had an embarrassed look.

Just as Susan was hoping that the session would end, Bill announced that they would have a math lesson. All students were given an assignment sheet with a puzzle about a bee flying back and forth between two trains approaching each other. Susan stared at the sheet and found herself unable to concentrate. She was not responding to her task in the role of a grade-school child but in the real-life role of a graduate student who was getting defensive about a silly activity. When a number of hands popped up excitedly, Susan began to panic. Bill, as the teacher, began making some sarcastic remarks about dumb kids, and she was getting ready to attack him. But, instead, she appealed to Dr. Dormer: "I don't know what this microteaching is supposed to demonstrate, but I find myself feeling very stupid and sorry. I don't think this is a useful task and I don't like the way Bill is picking on me . . ."

Bill looked a little embarrassed and was about to say something when Dr. Dormer stepped in with an apology. She explained that the whole thing was a set-up job to make some of the students experience what it feels like to be treated as a slow kid in a classroom full of faster ones. Bill, the teacher, was instructed to set up a high level of competition and to maintain a fast pace. He was asked to emphasize the differences by overly praising the fast finishers and making sarcastic comments about the slow ones. In reality, the speed with which different students broke the code or solved the puzzle had no relationship to their "smartness" because half of the class had additional clues in terms of the key word for the code or a hint about the flight of the bee.

The rest of the class session was spent in everyone sharing their feelings about the experience. Susan was surprised to find how many other "slower" students experienced her feelings and attempted to explain their slowness or to question the value of the exercise. Most of the slower students were resentful toward the teacher, while the faster ones went through the phases of personal delight and sympathy for the others. The class also spent some time trying to relate their experiences and emotions with those of a typical third grader. Just before the session came to an end, Dr. Dormer assigned a series of articles about the sociological system in the elementary school classrooms and the plight of children who are labeled as mentally retarded.

When the class met again the next Thursday, the effects of the experience were still there. The students brainstormed various techniques for reducing the plight of the slower child in the classroom through the use of individualized instruction. Susan felt that the level of participation in the project was one of the most active she had experienced in that course. She knew that her own interest and commitment were in large part due to the experience of having been a dumb kid.

EXAMPLE 2: FABULOUS CHICKENS

That was the last day of Dave's first month as the Assistant Manager of the local franchise of Fabulous Recipe Chickens. It was just a month ago that he completed the three-week course and came to this location. At the end of the course, he was given an experiential learning package which had an "experience card" for each day with a specific task to be completed on that day. For example, his task for that day was to talk to the counter attendants and find out what their major gripes were. The day before, he had to mingle

*unobtrusively with the customers and listen to their com-
ments. The day before that, he had to reconcile the cash
receipts with the register tapes twice during the day.*

*Dave had to complete his experiential exercises in addition
to carrying out his regular duties as the assistant manager. He
felt that he learned a lot about the day-to-day affairs of the
chicken place, but he wasn't sure exactly what he had
learned. He had a lot of unanswered questions, and his boss,
Mr. Caulton, was not much help in answering those. So it was
with a feeling of relief that Dave left for a one-day refresher
seminar in Fabulous Recipe Chickens' main office in Dayton.*

*At the seminar, Dave found eight other assistant managers
who had also worked through experiential exercises. In the
morning, they all met with Mark Garner, their trainer, who
explained that the entire seminar would be a "debriefing" of
their experiences. Mark went on to explain that his task was
merely to assist everyone in sharing their experiences. He
began by inviting the participants to report on any
frustration or hostility. After this gripe session, they all
settled down to some serious problem-solving. Helped by
Mark's skills as a group leader, the participants listed a
number of common problems and compared the different
solutions they had used. Dave was happy to discover a couple
of strategies which could be useful in his store, and he was
happier when some of the other participants praised one of
his solutions. During the last session of the day, all
participants had an opportunity to list their unanswered
questions and to figure out methods of getting them
answered.*

EXAMPLE 3: CHAUVINISTIC MALES

*The Leadership Workshop for women managers was
coming to an end and the last activity was a role play that
dealt with the topic of assertively handling chauvinist
colleagues.*

The participants were divided into groups of five, and each was given a different role card. An audiotape coordinated the role play by presenting the story, giving instructions, and timing the sessions. The first session was a departmental meeting. Mary played the role of a junior executive, and she was the only woman in the group, according to her role card. Carole got so much into her role as a male chauvinist supervisor that Mary was ready to kill her. Sandy had the role of a sympathetic departmental head, but Mary found "his" actions more patronizing than useful. Just as she was getting ready to throw a temper tantrum, the audiotape signaled the end of the session and changed the role-play situation.

The second session involved a discussion of whether or not the corporation should have a dress code. Mary was promoted to be the supervisor of another department, and she became a co-equal to the male chauvinist whose role Carole played. As the discussion got under way, Mary found herself disagreeing with Carole, not because she did not like the ideas, but because she still resented "his" chauvinistic behavior from the previous session. As could have been expected, the discussion became very heated before the audiotape signaled its end.

The tape now directed the participants to individually fill out a questionnaire. The questions dealt with people's perceptions of themselves and of others. Mary began answering them without any great enthusiasm, but she soon became interested when they referred back to her experiences and feelings from the role-play sessions. She was also reminded of several put-downs during her passage through the MBA course at the university just because she was female. After about 15 minutes, the voice on the audiotape suggested an open discussion of each item on the questionnaire, with the different participants taking turns to be the moderators. During the discussion, Mary was surprised at how many others had similar perceptions and feelings about the issue;

she was alarmed at the different strategies suggested for handling the basic male chauvinism at the office. The experience was definitely an eye-opener for everyone concerned.

The Experiential Learning Package as a Product

The three vignettes above show experiential learning packages in action. The descriptions are in terms of a *process,* and from the point of view of the consumers—either the learner or the instructor. Let's take another look at the three examples—this time at the *product* and from the point of view of an instructional designer.

All three packages have two different sections: the *experience* and the *debriefing.* In the *Stupid Students* example, the experiential section consisted of some instructions to the instructor on how to set up the fake microteaching sessions. This section included the lesson materials for microteaching. The debriefing section was also for the instructor. It contained a series of suggested questions for prompting the participants to explore their experiences and to become aware of their feelings and emotions. This section included a series of reference articles related to real-world classrooms.

The *Fabulous Chickens* example contained an experiential section in the form of 20 assignment cards. These cards required the learners to undergo a series of carefully selected and sequenced experiences. There was no need for an instructor in this section. The debriefing section depended on a leader. It contained a list of suggested questions to facilitate the sharing of the experiences when the different assistant managers were brought together for their one-day session. This leader's guide also contained a systematic procedure for debriefing which ensured that the participants discovered and evaluated their own solutions, rather than being told by the leader.

The *Chauvinistic Males* example uses the instructional design format known as *Rolemaps* (Dormant, 1980). The experience is structured by an audiotape which presents a simulated scenario. Even though it is a role play, the arguments, feelings, and emotions which it created were for real. The debriefing in this example was controlled by the audiotape and came in two stages. During the first stage, each person explored his or her own experiences using a structured set of questions. During the second stage, the participants in each group of five shared their personal perceptions and compared and contrasted their insights.

Learner Groups and Experiential Learning Packages

A more elaborate definition of the experiential learning package is provided in Chapter II. At this time, with the elementary examples and explanations above, we are ready to explore the uses of this instructional design.

While all types of learners can use experiential learning packages, some specific groups are likely to benefit more than others from this instructional design format. These groups are briefly described below.

The skeptics. You will find these learners in all walks of life, but mostly among alienated youths (such as high school dropouts). The skeptics are fond of citing the success stories of the self-taught and the horror stories of the college-educated. They have utter contempt for the value of formal education. Whether this contempt is justified or not, we cannot deny its existence. Any attempt to force people from this group into conventional classrooms or traditional training can only result in further alienation. Perhaps initial successes with experiential learning packages can eventually encourage them to explore more formal education.

The unsure. Many efficient students have the survival skills for coping with the classroom and scoring high on tests and examinations. However, contrary to what their test scores suggest, their confidence level in what they have learned (and its usefulness) remains very low. A dose of experiential learning may not boost their cognitive scores, but it may increase their belief in the strength and worth of their learning.

The nonverbal. Many intelligent people with nonverbal skills and intuitive knowledge remain unrecognized (or much worse, punished) in our formal educational systems. These learners cannot cope with the excessive verbal demands in traditional learning. They are not into reading or writing, nor do they have the patience to passively listen to a lecture based on the experience of others. Experiential learning packages offer an alternative approach for this group.

The excessively verbal. Excessively verbal learners can benefit from the enlightening effects of experiential learning packages for reasons that are different from those for the previous groups. Many learners who are reinforced in our school systems for their mastery of verbal knowledge mistakenly believe that they have all the answers. These learners equate their verbal knowledge of a definition to the ability to discriminate objects and events in the real world, and their rote recall of the steps of a procedure with its successful application to real-world problems. As may be predicted, these learners are usually painfully disillusioned when they find that their academic skills are no match for job requirements. Experiential learning packages in their educational process may tone down some of their unjustified arrogance and provide a welcome breath of fresh air.

Children. My primary interest in this book is in the application of experiential learning packages to *adult* learners. However, I should report the successful use of different types of experiential packages (including simulations and role plays) and standard debriefing procedures with grade-school children. Obviously, some adaptations have to be made to suit this type of learner, but I do not agree with a currently popular claim that experiential learning is "too heavy" for young children. The absurdity of this claim becomes apparent when we consider that experiential learning is the only kind of learning available to the infant. The fact that people complete more than 80 percent of all their total lifetime learning before the age of three bears testimony to the applicability of experiential learning packages to young learners.

Instructional Objectives and Experiential Learning Packages

Experiential learning packages are not equally useful for different types of instructional objectives. For example, you do not design such a package to teach basic facts such as dates in history. The instructional design appears to be most suited for the following types of objectives:

1. *Affective objectives.* No textbook chapter or lecture can evoke the feelings and emotions produced by actual participation in an intense experience. Both real-life experiences and their simulated representations produce lasting changes in the learner's values, beliefs, and attitudes. Susan's feelings as a stupid student in our first example are obviously more likely than a set of reference articles to change her attitudes.

2. *Empathic objectives.* A special type of affective objective involves appreciating what it feels like to be in another person's shoes. A simple learning experience of pretending to be a cripple and being pushed in a wheelchair around a shopping center makes one aware of the unconscious cruelty, patronizing, and repulsion with which handicapped people are treated in our society. Learners also experience the disillusionment and disenfranchisement of being a woman or a black or an Appalachian or a homosexual through the second-hand reality of role plays and simulations.

3. *Interactive objectives.* Experiential learning packages need not be limited to affective learning alone. There are

many cognitive skills—especially those related to human interaction—that are best learned in an experiential setting. You need suitable experiences to really acquire skills in interviewing, critical listening, counseling, and debriefing. Experiential learning packages can be effectively structured to enable the learner to perceive these interactions from both sides—as the listener and the speaker, as the guide and the follower, and as the challenger and the defender.

4. *Higher-level cognitive skills.* Experiential learning is especially useful for helping learners acquire and practice evaluation and synthesis skills. Real experiences provide us with realistic feedback that strengthens our ability to transfer and apply these skills to the outside world. Such experiences also provide the learner with confidence about the depth and worth of the learning.

5. *Unlearning objectives.* An irrational phobia and an unjustified prejudice are examples of undesirable affective and cognitive learning which require systematic unlearning. For example, I became aware of the number of my stereotypes about the typical American or the average housewife as a result of participating in simulation games. Although I pride myself on being broadminded, these experiences revealed subtle streaks of racism and male chauvinism. The debriefing sessions provided me with insights and procedures for unlearning my prejudices. In the affective domain, a number of current therapies are built around experiential learning. Systematic desensitization, for example, requires that you experience (and control) the fears and anxieties in different situations—first in your imagination and later in the real world. Many meek people have learned how to be more assertive through the experiences of a behavioral rehearsal in which they role play the action of returning damaged merchandise to the store and later actually experiencing the real activity. In all of these cases, structured series of experiences and careful debriefing bring about the unlearning of undesirable behaviors.

**Curriculum Areas, Educational Situations,
and Experiential Learning Packages**

We may extrapolate from the discussions of types of learners and instructional objectives to broader curriculum areas and educational contexts in which experiential learning packages are especially useful.

1. *Vocational training.* Experiential learning packages have more than face validity for job training and career education. Through field-based and simulated experiences, it is possible to bring the world of work closer to young learners. Such an approach provides more relevance to the curriculum and emphasizes important factors that are ignored in a purely academic approach. In specialized job areas, where the market is thin and training materials are not available, the experiential approach may be the most cost-effective method.

2. *Training in the helping professions.* Within the broad area of vocational training, experiential learning packages appear to be most suited for the preparation of such helping professionals as teachers, therapists, social workers, and medical technicians. Role plays and simulations can add relevance to this kind of training. They are especially useful for creating empathy for the receiver of the help. For example, social workers who have played the role of welfare recipients report that their perceptions and performances have been considerably changed through the experience. One sometimes wonders how valuable it would be to subject all physicians to the role of suffering patients during their professional training.

3. *Internship.* Doctors, lawyers, accountants, teachers, and sundry other professionals usually undergo an internship period. This type of internship is meant to provide valuable experience in supervised situations to the beginning professional. Very often, however, the experiences are not usefully organized; nor is any systematic debriefing undertaken to

assist the trainee in reflecting upon the experience and deriving useful insights and skills. Experiential learning packages may provide useful techniques for creating and sequencing suitable activities and for structuring the debriefing in these situations.

4. *Developing areas.* In countries and situations where the budget for education does not allow too many luxuries, superfluous training should be kept to a minimum. In many governmental projects, initial training is undertaken to "brief" trainees. A cost-effective alternative may be to let the people get on with their job and their experience and then receive debriefing to clarify specific problems. For example, much shotgun training and education on birth-control practices is wasted on people who do not have the necessary experiences to understand what is being "taught" to them. This approach can be effectively replaced by using incentives to encourage an exploration of birth-control, and then providing meaningful debriefing related to individual problems.

5. *Reducing trauma.* Life is full of painful experiences that may be individually unpredictable but are collectively predictable. Sooner or later, every family goes through a death in its midst. A part of the population suffers from fires, floods, highway accidents, and rape. These painful experiences leave deep scars along with useful and useless changes in attitudes and behaviors. They also present opportunities for individual growth toward greater self-reliance and realistic trust of others. The technique of experiential learning package development—especially that of creating debriefing procedures—can offer useful guidelines for utilizing the learning opportunities inherent in these ready-made experiences. For example, a standardized debriefing procedure for use by social workers and law offices with rape victims will contribute immensely to learning from the trauma and the unlearning of exaggerated fears or grief.

Some Caveats

The design, development, and use of an experiential learning package require heavy commitments of time and other resources. It is a much more complex instructional design than, for example, programmed instruction. It is important that the topic and the objective be selected very carefully, if we are to obtain maximum returns for our investment in this design format. Here are some caveats about situations where the use of experiential learning packages is *not* recommended.

1. *Rote learning of factual materials.* It is possible to teach librarians about different types of catalog cards through a series of experiential assignments. However, this type of pseudo-discovery approach is very inefficient when compared to telling them the information or providing them with a listing. Many instructional tasks are so simple that the use of this experiential learning would be a waste. These packages are definitely not recommended for such simple factual learning.

2. *Highly complex-cognitive tasks.* Just as this instructional design format is unsuited for simple tasks, it is also unsuited for very complex ones. Abstract, symbolic cognitive skills (e.g., differential calculus, symbolic logic, or transformational grammar) belong to this category. Even in less abstract areas, complex cognitive tasks may have to be split into simpler ones for initial training before an integrating experience is provided. It is worth remembering that experiential learning packages are more suited to providing *practice* than initial instruction.

3. *Untrained trainers and immature learners.* Experiential learning packages which are designed for affective objectives require specialist trainers and mature learners. In the hands of an inexperienced instructor, the activity described in the first example may result in unpleasant consequences. Even in the hands of an expert trainer, this activity may backfire if the

learners are hostile toward each other. The design of experiential learning packages in controversial, affective areas may be better left aside until you have gained experience in designing less critical exercises.

4. *Uneasy designers.* A number of ethical questions confront the designer of experiential learning packages. Two major issues among these are the following:

• We are being selective when we structure different experiences and the debriefing questions. These actions introduce our own bias in the learning outcomes. To what extent are we justified in doing this? And to what extent is our distortion of "reality" likely to damage the learner?

• In creating many of our experiences, we may use various ruses. In most simulation activities, the learner, the instructor, and the outsiders all know that we are pretending and agree to do that. But in a few other types of experiences, we consciously hide some aspect of reality, either from the learners or from the outsiders. In the *Stupid Students* example, we hid the fact that some students are given an extra advantage, while the others are made to feel slow and incompetent. In a typical assertiveness-training exercise, we require the student to buy some merchandise with the full intent of returning it to the store, for no reason whatsoever. In the *Assume a Handicap* exercise, we may push a healthy learner in a wheelchair so that he or she can experience the typical reactions of the general public. You may have concerns about the morality of the use of these strategies. While I have my own personal guidelines about the extent to which I am willing to simulate and dissimulate for instructional purposes, I do not have a universal code of ethics. If you are planning to prepare an experiential learning package with strategies that involve some moral choices, I recommend an excellent book on lying by Sisseal Bok (1978) and a lot of personal soul-searching. I would also like to suggest that you steer away from such strategies until you have had considerable experience in designing, using, and debriefing simpler packages.

Summary

An experiential learning package is designed to help people learn from their experiences. It consists of an experience section and a debriefing section. This instructional design format is especially suited for use with learners who are skeptical or unsure about what they are learning and with learners who have insufficient or excessive verbal fluency. Experiential learning packages help learners to effectively attain affective, empathic, interactive, and complex cognitive objectives. They also help people unlearn undesirable cognitive prejudices and affective anxieties. Experiential learning packages are especially recommended for vocational education in the helping professions and in instructional situations that involve internships. They are also used to create debriefing components to help learners after personal trauma. Very simple or very complex cognitive tasks are not appropriate for this format. The beginning designer is advised to avoid controversial content and questionable strategies.

References

Bok, S. *Lying: Moral Choice in Public and Private Life.* New York: Pantheon Books, 1978.

Dormant, D. *Rolemaps.* Englewood Cliffs, New Jersey: Educational Technology Publications, 1980.

II.

OPERATIONAL DESCRIPTION

We briefly explored three experiential learning packages in the first chapter, and they all contained an experiential section and debriefing section. We are now ready to take a closer look at this instructional design to identify its critical attributes. We shall also examine the various ways in which one experiential learning package may differ from another.

Critical Attributes of
an Experiential Learning Package

The experiential learning package specifies a relevant experience and provides a procedure for analyzing this experience to help the learner achieve a specific instructional goal.

The four critical attributes of experiential learning packages are discussed below:

It is a package. Because we are interested in the design of an instructional material rather than extemporaneous teaching, we want to emphasize that the experiential learning *package* is a tangible product. We use this term to refer specifically to the instructional material rather than to the methodology in general.

Later in this chapter, we will describe how the physical nature of one package may differ from that of another.

It has a specific instructional goal. Both sections of the experiential learning package are directly designed to help the learner achieve a specific instructional goal. Later in this chapter, we will see how this goal may relate to different domains of learning. At this time, it is important to remember that both the experience and the debriefing are related to this instructional goal.

It includes a relevant experience. The experiential learning package contains an experience, or more specifically, instructions to the learners on how to undergo an experience (or instructions to their leader on how to provide such an experience). Because everything you do during your waking hours (or for that matter, even during your sleep) may be termed an "experience," we need to define more closely what we mean by this term. To do this, we must first specify our instructional objective. For example, let's imagine that our objective is for the learner *to tell jokes.* Reading a book on how to tell a joke, or watching a videotape demonstration by a comedian, or listening to a lecture of joke-telling are all experiences—and relevant ones at that. But these are didactic experiences whose content is only *related* to our instructional objective. In an experiential learning package, the relevant experience we are talking about is a *direct* experience of the *content* of our instructional objective.

The experiential section of our joke-telling package may contain this instruction:

On the following page, you will find ten jokes. Read all of them and select the one you like best. Without referring to the page, tell this joke to a friend.

This is not the experience either, but *specifications* for it. The learner undergoes the actual, relevant experience when he or she *tells the joke to someone.*

Can listening to a lecture, watching a television program, or reading a book ever become a relevant experience according to our definition? It can, in some specific cases. For example, if the instructional objective deals with selective reading, then reading a textbook (any textbook) becomes a relevant experience. If the instructional objective is to stay awake during a lecture, then listening to a lecture could be a relevant experience. Similarly, if we are interested in teaching how television commercials persuade us, then watching television becomes a relevant experience.

Later in this chapter, we will see how the experiences in different packages may vary in their degree of structure, role of learners, interaction among learners, and the role of the leader.

It includes a debriefing section. The debriefing section helps the learner to reflect on the experience in order to achieve the instructional objectives for the package. Therefore, it is directly related to the instructional goals (and also to the experience).

For example, the debriefing section for our joke-telling package may require the learner to answer a set of questions such as the following:

---

1. What was your friend's reaction to your joke? Did he or she laugh? Did that make you feel good? Did he or she fail to laugh? Did that make you feel stupid?

2. How closely did you stick to the original joke? Did you memorize it? Or, did you come up with your own variation?

3. How do you think you could improve your joke-telling ability?

Later in this chapter, we will see how the debriefing section in different packages may differ in its degree of structure, role of learners, interaction among learners, and the role of the leader.

Variable Attributes of Experiential Learning Packages

All experiential learning packages should have the four critical attributes listed above. But, within these broad constraints, they may vary in a number of different ways to suit the specific needs. In this section of the chapter, we will explore variations in the following five areas:

(1) variations in packaging;

(2) variations in instructional goals;

(3) variations in the relationship between the experience and the debriefing;

(4) variations in the experiential section; and

(5) variations in the debriefing section.

Variations in Packaging

Experiential learning packages are tangible products, but they come in all sizes and use different media. One of my quick samples is printed on a 3 x 5 index card. Instructions for the experience are on one side:

Draw straight, connected lines that go through all nine dots, but through each dot only once. The object is to see how few lines you use:

The debriefing instructions are on the other side:

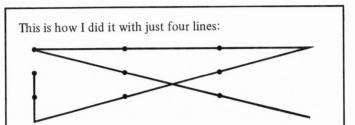

This is how I did it with just four lines:

Did you fail to come up with the solution because you assumed that the lines should not go beyond the dots? Take a couple of minutes to think about all other unnecessary assumptions made. And then see if you can solve the puzzle with just three lines . . .

In contrast to this "micro" package, another experiential learning package on teacher training comes as a complex media production. A computer controlled film projection device begins by showing a scene from a classroom. The film stops at a critical juncture and requires the viewer to play the role of the teacher to solve the problem. The teacher is given four options to choose from and indicates the choice by pushing a button. The computer selects the appropriate branch of the film, screens the consequence of the teacher's action, and proceeds to the next critical incident. This process is repeated a number of times before the viewer is debriefed.

Other experiential learning packages use videotape and audiotape recordings, microcomputer programs, sound slide sets, and multimedia kits. But the majority of effective packages are limited to the printed page (which directs the learner's interaction with the whole outside world).

Variations in Instructional Goals

Experiential learning packages are designed to achieve various types of goals: affective, cognitive, and psychomotor.

However, as we indicated earlier, this instructional design format is best suited for the following types of goals:

1. *Affective goals*: E.g., "Acquire a positive attitude toward assertive behavior."

2. *Empathic goals*: E.g., "Become aware of the complex feelings of a technical assistance provider working in a developing nation."

3. *Interactive goals*: E.g., "Demonstrate active listening skills in counseling a troubled adolescent."

4. *Higher-level cognitive goals*: E.g., "Solve real-life management problems using Theory Z."

5. *Unlearning goals*: E.g., "Reduce personal anxiety level about public speaking."

Earlier, we also suggested that experiential learning packages are not particularly suited for lower-level cognitive goals, abstract goals, and affective goals which involve moral decisions.

Experiential packages are very effective in helping learners achieve psychomotor goals. Actually, you cannot learn to swim or to drive a car without an experiential component. However, the strategies and principles required for designing a psychomotor package are much different from those required for affective and cognitive ones. Because of this, we do not discuss psychomotor packages in this book.

*Variations in the Relationship Between
the Experience and the Debriefing*

Time lag. In some experiential learning packages, the debriefing activity immediately follows the experiential activity. For example, your learners play a 15-minute simulation game and you spend the next 30 minutes of the class period debriefing them. In other experiential packages, there is a significant delay between the experience and the debriefing activity. For example, during a training lecture on police methods, a violent fight takes place outside the classroom—but clearly visible to the learners. The trainer does not comment upon this event immediately; but, during another lecture a month later, he or she recalls the incident and debriefs the trainees to demonstrate variations among different eye-witness reports—especially after the lapse of a long period of time.

In the example above, the time lag was built into the experience to serve an instructional purpose. Usually, however, whether or not debriefing immediately follows the experience depends upon scheduling factors. A rule of thumb is to debrief the learners immediately following the experiential activity, unless there is some instructional reason(s) for not doing so.

Relative proportion. A sample experiential learning package involves a group of learners drawing lines to connect consecutive numbers which are randomly scattered all over a worksheet. In this adaptation of Ruben and Budd's (1978) exercise, the learners do this activity three times, each time working for exactly 20 seconds. This one-minute experiential activity is then debriefed during the next three hours! (Although all learners apparently use the same worksheet and receive the same instructions, this is not so.) The resulting differences are explored during the debriefing session to derive principles about various factors that influence human performance: experience, motivation, positive and negative transfer of training, clarity of objectives, irrelevant stimuli, unnecessary responses, amount of feedback, and background knowledge.

In contrast to the example above, a lengthy exercise in an assertiveness package requires relaxing oneself while visualizing increasingly tense situations. This experiential session lasts for a couple of hours spread over a period of three weeks. No debriefing follows this experience, unlike most packages, because the instructional point (that you could consciously relax even in a tense situation) has been made during the experience itself.

The relative proportions of the experience and debriefing may vary from one package to another. If there is a rule of thumb in this area, it is that the debriefing session should last as long as (and no longer than) you are able to derive useful learning from the experience.

Timing of debriefing. In general, the debriefing section comes at the end of the entire experiential activity. However, when the experience is a lengthy one, or if it consists of a series of graduated exercises, it may be a good idea to debrief at the end of each unit rather than wait for the completion of all of them. This ensures that the experience is still fresh in the learners' memories. Also, you may use the same questions during different debriefing sessions to facilitate systematic comparison.

Variations in the Experiential Section

Degree of simulation. Some experiential learning packages stick to reality, while others use some degree of simulation. For example, when you ask the trainee to work at the real cash register in a shop, this experiential activity involves reality. But when you ask the trainee to play the role of an employee at the cash register being unjustly accused of short-changing a customer, the experiential activity involves simulation.

Simulations provide different advantages in experiential learning packages: They offer a greater degree of control, reduce physical and emotional risks, and ensure critical incidents within a given time frame. However, unless carefully designed, the simulation may miss some critical elements of reality and lose the impact of experiential learning. The more abstract the simulation, the less powerful it becomes. For example, a mathematical formula simulates the realities of traffic flow through a busy intersection. However, a symbolic manipulation of this formula is more like formal, verbal learning than an experiential episode.

A rule of thumb in designing simulations is to retain reality to the maximum extent possible without making the experience risky or inefficient.

Degree of dissimulation. Related to simulation is the degree of dissimulation, which deals with any "secrets" in the procedure. A powerful experiential package, noted earlier, for acquiring empathy for the handicapped requires the learner to assume a handicap. For example, this learner may travel in a wheelchair in a public building, pretending to be crippled. People in this building are deceived into believing that the learner is really crippled and behave in a natural manner toward him or her, providing an authentic experience.

One of our earlier vignettes (STUPID STUDENTS) illustrates another level of dissimulation. In this case, the instructor and some students know what is happening, but important information is withheld from other learners. These learners feel stupid to a degree which is impossible to achieve through an "open" simulation in which everyone *knows* it is all "make believe."

Our rule of thumb in this area repeats an earlier warning: *proceed with caution*; be sure that the results warrant your deception and the loss of your credibility. Also, make sure that all secret information is revealed to all learners during the debriefing session.

Degree of structure. The experiential section may be tightly organized and specify to the learner what to do, whom to see, and what to say at what time. In addition, it may program the leader into presenting the experience. In contrast, other packages may encourage open-ended experiences by providing such general instructions as "Drive around the poor section of town between 3 a.m. and 4 a.m. tomorrow." One of my favorite examples takes this type of openness one step further. It is a booklet for newlyweds with this instruction on the cover page: "Do not open until after your first *serious* fight." (When the couple does open the booklet, they find a series of debriefing questions to reflect on the causes of the conflict and potential ways of avoiding its recurrence.)

Role of learners. Most experiential packages require learners to actively participate in the experience and permit them to behave in their natural manner. A few others require learners to passively experience what is happening (e.g., at 3 a.m. in the downtown area) without such active participation. In all cases, however, the experience is designed to be intensely involving, and the learner is not required to self-consciously process what is happening to him or her.

Interaction among learners. Some experiential packages are designed for use by a single learner acting alone, while others involve a group. Within the group, learners may operate at different levels of interaction:

- *Parallel activity*: In this experience, all learners undertake the same type of activity but independently of each other. This experience could have been carried out individually, except group work results in more divergent data for debriefing.
- *Team activity*: In this experience, a small group of learners undertakes a collaborative activity, each performing a different role. For example, one learner pretends to be blind while another leads him or her by the hand.
- *Complementary activity*: In this experience, different learners interact with one another in complementary roles. For example, one learner assumes the role of a supervisor negotiating with a group of technical workers whose roles are played by the other learners. In another example, learners pair up to practice interrogation techniques. In these complementary experiences, all learners usually get to play all roles. Thus, at the end of the assigned time, the police

officer and the suspect may change their roles and re-enact the same interrogation scene.

Role of the leader. Some experiential packages are self-instructional, while others require a leader. Our earlier vignette, CHAUVINISTIC MALES, is a self-instructional package which involves a group of learners. An audiotape controls the simulated experiential activity. In the FABU-LOUS CHICKENS vignette, the experiential section is once again self-instructional (although the debriefing is not). In contrast, in the STUPID STUDENTS vignette, the experience is heavily dependent on the leader. He or she not only transmits the instructions on what to do, but also carefully orchestrates the experience, which involves a high degree of both simulation and dissimulation.

We have seen the different ways in which the experiential section of a learning package may vary. Below, we will explore the variations in the debriefing section, using the same dimensions as far as possible.

Variations in the Debriefing Section

Degree of structure. The debriefing section of the experiential package may be tightly structured to contain a series of specific activities and questions for the learners. It may also program the leader's behavior by listing the questions to be asked in a prearranged sequence. In contrast, this section could be left open-ended and merely suggest that the learners share their experiences.

The degree of structure of the debriefing section is also related to its relationship to the instructional goals of the package. A *goal-based debriefing* section contains a set of questions directly related to each specific objective of the package. In contrast, a *goal-free debriefing* section contains questions related to all aspects of the experience whether they deal with the instructional goals of the package or not.

Role of learners. Most debriefing sections require active, overt participation from learners, who are required to write down responses to questions or to discuss different topics with one another. Other debriefing sections involve the passive experience of listening to a short lecture on relevant concepts from the leader. Most of our examples are of the active-participation type. Only in some special situations may the debriefing section tend toward the passive side.

Interaction among learners. Some debriefing sections are designed for independent use by individual learners. This type of debriefing is especially suitable when it is important to protect the privacy of the learners. When debriefing is designed for group use, it may be in any one of the following forms:

- *Parallel activity*: In this type of debriefing, the group serves a nominal role and merely increases the amount of information to be analyzed. All learners respond to the same set of questions, but there is no interaction among them.
- *Interactive activity*: In this type of debriefing, learners collaboratively respond to questions. They share their experiences and compare and contrast what happened to them individually.
- *Complementary activity*: In this type of debriefing, different learners take the lead in debriefing the group. For example, different learners may take turns being the moderators (and reporters) during the discussion of different topics. Pairs of learners may also facilitate the debriefing process by asking each other suitable questions and sharing their experiences.

Role of the leader. It is possible to design the debriefing section to directly involve the learners without the intervention of a leader. Usually, however, the leader has a greater role to play in the debriefing section than in the experiential section. In some debriefing, the leader plays the role of an *expert* and builds upon the learners' experiences to explain relevant principles from a subject-matter area. In contrast to this, in other debriefings, the leader plays a neutral facilitator role. In this role, he or she merely asks questions and keeps the group focused on the discussion.

We have frequently presented two extreme poles to illustrate different dimensions of debriefing (and of experiencing). It should be obvious that many other levels exist within these extremes. This is what makes experiential learning packages a flexible and powerful instructional design format.

Summary

A summary of this chapter is given as a definition table (see Figure 1).

In addition to reminding you of the critical points discussed in this chapter, this Figure can give you a checklist for your experiential learning package. You will also find this Figure handy in analyzing any existing experiential package.

Reference

Ruben, B.D., and R.W. Budd. Numbers: A Problem-Solving Activity. In J. W. Pfeiffer and J.E. Jones (Eds.), *The 1978 Annual Handbook for Group Facilitators.* La Jolla, California: University Associates, 1978.

Figure 1

Definitions of Terms

EXPERIENTIAL LEARNING PACKAGES

Definition: An experiential learning package is an instructional material that specifies a relevant experience and provides a procedure for analyzing this experience to help the learners achieve a specific instructional goal.

Critical   • It is a package, rather than a method.
attributes: • It has a specific instructional goal.
                      • It includes a relevant experience.
                      • It includes a debriefing section.

Variable   • The package may be of any size and use any
attributes: media.
                      • The goals of the package may be affective,
                        cognitive, or psychomotor.
                      • The debriefing activity may immediately
                        follow the experience or be delayed.
                      • The relative proportion of the experience
                        and the debriefing may vary.
                      • The debriefing activity may be interspersed
                        after convenient units of the experience or
                        reserved until the end of the entire experience.
                      • The degree of simulation and dissimulation
                        of the experience may vary.
                      • Different pieces of information may be
                        withheld from different people during the
                        experience.
                      • The experience may be tightly or loosely
                        structured through instructions to the learners and/or their leaders.

(Continued on Next Page)

Figure 1 (Continued)

- The experience may require various amounts of active participation from the learners.
- The experience may involve different degrees of interaction among the learners.
- The role of the leader in presenting or facilitating the experience may vary.
- The debriefing section may be tightly or loosely structured through instructions to learners and/or to their leaders.
- Debriefing questions may be limited to those aspects of the experience that are directly related to the instructional goal or expanded to all aspects of the experience.
- Debriefing may require various degrees of active participation from the learners.
- Debriefing may involve different degrees of interaction among the learners.
- The role of the leader during debriefing may be that of a subject-matter expert or of a neutral facilitator.

III.

DESIGN FORMAT

In the first chapter of this book, we indicated that an experiential learning package includes two major parts: the experience and a debriefing. In the second chapter, we introduced a number of critical and variable attributes related to the design format of experiential learning packages. In this chapter, we provide another framework for analyzing the physical components of an experiential package. We apply this framework to the analysis of the three earlier example vignettes and a new, fourth one. We then discuss in some detail the design format of the debriefing section.

Components of an Experiential Package

Figure 2 graphically illustrates the different components of an experiential package in terms of the materials for the learners and their leaders. In the first level, the package is divided into the experiential and debriefing sections. In the second level, each of these sections is divided into materials for learners and materials for the leader. Both of these types of materials are further divided into "instructions" and "other materials." "Instructions" specify a procedure: They direct the learner or the leader to do certain things in a certain sequence. "Other materials" contain the content which provides the learners and the leader with background information or facilitates the experiential and the debriefing activities.

37

Figure 2

Components of an Experiential Learning Package

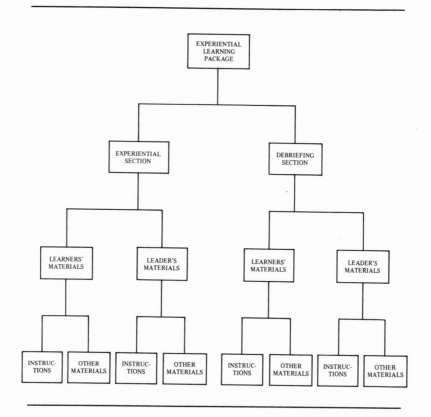

The nature and functions of these components become clearer when we apply them to the three vignettes from the first chapter. As you can see from these analyses, not all experiential packages contain all of these components.

Example 1: STUPID STUDENTS

EXPERIENTIAL SECTION

Instructions to the leader:	This section spells out the details of setting up two fake microteaching sessions. The instructions specify how to select a learner to play the role of the teacher and how to select the victims to be portrayed as the "stupid students." It also gives information on training the learner who is to be the "teacher." Part of the role of the leader is delegated to the person playing the role of the teacher. Instructions to this teacher include how to teach the lessons on deciphering and mathematics and how to create an intense feeling of being "dumb" on the part of the selected "victims."
Other materials for the leader:	These include all background information related to the experience (i.e., deciphering secret messages and the mathematics puzzle). These materials are shared by the leader and the person playing the role of the teacher.
Instructions to the learners:	Instructions to the learners are supplied by the "teacher" in the simulated microteaching session. These instructions require the learners to decipher a coded message during the first session and to solve a mathematical puzzle during the second.

Other materials for the learners:	These include the various worksheets supplied to the learners during the two sessions. Although they all look the same (a coded message in the first one and a mathematical puzzle in the second), the worksheets for the selected victims do not contain the essential clues (i.e., the key word in the first case and a hint about the flight of the bee in the second case).

DEBRIEFING SECTION

Instructions to the leader:	This section provides detailed instructions about when to stop the experiential activity, when to reveal the secret information, how to encourage expression of learners' feelings and emotions, how to handle possible outbursts from the "stupid students," and how to explore various effects of labeling.
Other materials for the leader:	The debriefing section for the leader also contains a set of questions and sample comments to elicit various principles related to the effects of labeling students. A number of reference papers on this topic are included to provide the leader with relevant background information.
Instructions to the learners:	These are provided through the leader. They encourage the learners to express their feelings and to discuss a set of questions on the basis of their experiences and from the point of view of a typical third grader in an elementary school.
Other materials for the learners:	A series of reference articles on the sociological system in elementary school classrooms.

Example 2: FABULOUS CHICKENS

EXPERIENTIAL SECTION

Instructions to the leader:	A few simple instructions are given to the leader who conducts the initial three-week course for assistant managers. The instructions require him or her to hand out an "experience-card" packet to each trainee during the last day and explain that they are on-the-job assignments to be completed.

Other materials for the leader:	None. However, the leader is expected to be familiar with the contents of the experience cards.

Instructions to the learners:	General instructions are provided by the leader and repeated on an introductory card. Specific instructions for each day's experiential assignment are printed on individual cards. They specify the assignment in fairly open-ended terms (e.g., "Mingle anonymously with your customers and listen to their complaints.").

Other materials for the learners:	A few questionnaires are included in the packet for note-taking purposes. The learners are also provided with various forms and checklists related to the job (e.g., form for reconciling the cash register balance and a checklist of monthly supplies).

DEBRIEFING SECTION

Instructions to the leader:	This section provides detailed instructions to the leader on how to be a neutral facilitator. The guidelines suggest that the leader should first explain the goals and procedures for the debriefing section and then clear the air by

encouraging trainee complaints about their experiences. This is to be followed by a series of problem-solving sessions.

Other materials   This section includes some sample problems
for the leader: and solutions from the previous groups.

Instructions   These are provided by the leader.
to the learners:

Other materials   The learners use various forms for defining their
for the   problems and recording their solutions. They
learners: also have access to reference materials on the
                         fast-food industry and the official procedures
                         manual from the company.

Example 3: CHAUVINISTIC MALES

EXPERIENTIAL SECTION

Materials for   None, because this is designed to be a self-con-
the leader: tained package for direct use by the learners.
                         However, any leader who plans to use the
                         package should become familiar with the con-
                         tent and the method.

Instructions   General instructions are provided by an audio-
to the   tape recording. These structure the entire role-
learners: play activity and keep time. Specific role
                         assignments and instructions on how to play
                         the role are provided through individual role
                         cards.

Other materials for the learners:	The background story for each role-play session is provided by the narration on the tape. Simulated company memos are distributed to each learner.

DEBRIEFING SECTION

Materials for the leader:	None. However, as in the case of the experiential section, any leader who plans to use the package should become familiar with its content and method.

Instructions to the learners:	Debriefing instructions are provided by the audiotape recording. It directs the learners to individually fill out a questionnaire. After 15 minutes, the tape suggests a discussion of each item on the questionnaire with different learners taking turns to be moderators.

Other materials for the learners:	Individual copies of the questionnaire which relate the outcomes of the role-play session to male chauvinism in real-world offices.

Another Example for Analysis

Let's take one more example of an experiential learning package and analyze its design format both in terms of its components (as we did above) and in terms of the critical and variable attributes presented in the Operational Description chapter.

EXAMPLE 4: JOINT VENTURE

The instructional goal of this experiential learning package is to explore the formation of coalitions. It is a simulation game designed to relate individual resources, previous experiences, and the amount of payoffs to the rapidity of coalition formation and the degree of individual satisfaction.

Here is the game in action as used by my friend Diane in a workshop session:

The group of 21 participants are divided into three groups of five and one of six and seated around separate tables. Diane plunks down play money to the amount of $2000 in the middle of each table and announces that it is the payoff for the first round of the game. She also gives five playing cards (A-5 of the same suit) to the people at each table (and six to the last table) and asks them to be randomly distributed. She announces that each player is a small-business entrepreneur and the cards represent his or her total resources (e.g., assets, number of staff members, years of experience in the field, equipment, etc.). The players are interested in undertaking a large-scale project with the specified payoff ($2000 for this round). However, no single entrepreneur has sufficient resources to bid for the project. Therefore, it is necessary for two or more players to form a coalition before being awarded the contract.

Diane declares that for the first round of the game, the minimum resource requirement is eight units. If any number of players (within each group) can show her cards with a total value of at least eight and agree on a plan to divide the $2000, then they can share the payoff immediately according to their formula.

Different tables are at different levels of confusion as players attempt to figure out the mechanics of the game and to negotiate with each other. In one group, John and Mary, with 5 and 3 on their cards, decide immediately to form a coalition. The others in that group team up against them, but they soon discover that their cards add up to only seven. In the meantime, John wants to divide the money according to the ratio of their assets so that he gets $1250 and Mary gets

$750. But Mary thinks that the money should be split 50-50. While this argument goes on, the players with the A and the 2 talk among themselves and offer to split the money proportionately if John dumps Mary and takes them as partners. Mary does not like this undercutting strategy, but before she says anything, John agrees to the new offer. They go to Diane with their cards and their formula.

After about five minutes, when the slowest team makes up its mind, Diane announces the second round. The cards are mixed up and redistributed at each table. Diane explains that this round is just like the previous one, except for two modifications: The payoff is $5000, and there is a two-minute time limit. If any group does not have its coalition formed at the end of this time, the money will go back to the treasury. Negotiations begin immediately at each table. One of the groups does not come up with a coalition, and Diane takes back their money.

The next two rounds are played just about the same way, except the payoff increases to $10,000 and the minimum resources are raised to **nine**. *The time limit for the third round is two minutes and for the fourth, one minute! One of the groups decides to pool all of the resources and share the $10,000 evenly during these two rounds. People at the other tables go through sorting out offers and counteroffers.*

Diane now announces the fifth round and explains that it will be the last one. She emphasizes that the player with the most money at the end of this round is declared the winner. There is to be a winner for each group and a grand champion who has the highest amount among all groups. This round results in much more bargaining before it comes to an end.

Diane declares a coffee break, but the players are too eager to find out who won. So she asks everyone to count their total winnings. There is a low hubbub for a few minutes, and then each group announces its winner amidst boos and *cheers. The "commonwealth" group proudly announces that everyone at their table won, but their winning amount is the smallest one. The grand champion is John with an accumulated wealth of $21,005.*

Now the players are willing to take their coffee break. Diane skims through the debriefing manual and takes some notes. When the players come back after 15 minutes, she says, "During the play of the game and right now I feel a lot of emotions. Let's focus on these feelings and see if you want to share them. You may want to close your eyes and get in touch with these feelings. After some time, if you want to share your feelings with the others, feel free to make a statement. However, you do not have to, if you don't want to." There is a long silence and some uneasy squirming. Diane decides to get things rolling by expressing some of her own feelings. She says, "I felt sorry for the player who had a 2 during three consecutive rounds. Nobody seemed to negotiate with him." Alan confesses that he is that person and that he felt angry over the luck of the deal and decided it was a silly game! One member of the "commonwealth" group reports that she felt very close to the other members of her group because they all decided to share and share alike. Another member of the same group, however, reports that he resented the group pressure to conform and he is glad the game is over. This statement provokes some personal attacks, but Diane steps in tactfully and refocuses the group on their feelings rather than on the causes of these feelings.

After about ten minutes of clearing the air, Diane launches into the second phase of debriefing. She reminds the group about the objectives for the exercise and announces that she is going to systematically collect experiences about various aspects of coalition behavior. Through a series of skillful questions, she elicits some basic principles about people's eagerness to form coalitions and their satisfaction derived from the activity. She relates each principle to the learners' real-world experiences.

The debriefing lasts for about 40 minutes, and although a couple of people get fidgety, most seem to be enjoying themselves and learning. It is about ten o'clock when the session comes to an end.

Let's analyze JOINT VENTURE in terms of its components as we did with the three earlier examples.

EXPERIENTIAL SECTION

Instructions to the leader:	The game leader's manual contains detailed instructions on assembling the game materials, dividing the total group into smaller groups, and conducting each round of the game.

Other materials for the leader:	A brief introduction to the leader's manual provides background information on the instructional goals of the simulation game and a brief history of the systematic design and development procedure. The Appendix to the manual contains reprints of some theoretical articles on the social psychology of coalition formation.

Instructions to the learners:	The package contains the rules of the game printed on a single sheet of paper, ready to be duplicated and distributed to individual learners (although, in our example, Diane chose not to use it).

Other materials for the learners:	Materials used during the game such as playing cards and play money.

DEBRIEFING SECTION

Instructions to the leader:	There is a comprehensive set of instructions to the leader on how to debrief the learners. (These instructions are very similar to those provided later in this chapter.)
Other materials for the leader:	The leader's manual contains a number of suggested debriefing questions (e.g., "Did the coalitions during later rounds form faster than those in earlier ones?") and summaries of research findings related to each of these questions.
Instructions to the learners:	These are provided by the leader, based on the instructions given to him or her.
Other materials for the learners:	After the conclusion of the debriefing session, the learners are given a reprint of an article on the social psychology of coalition formation.

Let's now analyze JOINT VENTURE once again—this time in terms of the variable attributes listed in Figure 1.

Packaging variables: The basic core of the package is a leader's guide of 30 pages. The leader collects (or creates) play money and playing cards locally. There is a master copy of the rules of the game to be duplicated and distributed to the players.

Instructional goals: The instructional goals for the package are primarily cognitive; they involve exploring various causes and effects related to coalition formation. There is also an affective, empathic goal dealing with the feelings of power and powerlessness during the formation of coalitions.

Relationship between the experience and the debriefing: The debriefing activity follows the experience after a short break. The experience lasts for about 30 minutes while the debriefing goes on for 40 minutes. Although the experience is divided into five rounds (each with some systematic variation), the debriefing is reserved until the end of the final round so that players have more data to compare and contrast.

Degree of simulation: This experiential activity involves a rather abstract simulation. Although a scenario dealing with small-business entrepreneurs is used, the topic being simulated is the process of coalition formation.

Degree of dissimulation: No piece of information is purposely withheld from any player during the experiential activity. However, information about the conditions for each round and the total number of rounds is not revealed until the last moment (in order to discourage any long-term strategies).

Tightness of structure: The experience is tightly structured because it is in the form of a game. The rules control the relative resources for each player, the amount of payoff, the nature of negotiations, and the time limits.

Degree of active participation: The game encourages a high level of active participation among the players. The small number of players in each group, time limits, and the motivating effect of the payoff—all of these require this active participation.

Degree of interaction: The degree of interaction during the experiential activity is very high because its content— coalition formation—is an interactive process. This is not a game for solitaire play.

Role of the leader during the experience: The leader plays an important role in the experiential section. Although not a part of the experience itself, he or she coordinates the logistics of the game, announces new rules and constraints, distributes resources, sets up time limits, and makes sure that the rules are being followed.

Structure of the debriefing section: Debriefing is tightly structured with comprehensive instructions. In addition, sample questions which are directly related to the instructional goals are provided to the leader.

Active participation and interaction during debriefing: The debriefing section requires active, interactive participation. The leader asks questions but does not supply the answers. Different participants offer opinions from their experiences and jointly derive general principles about coalition formation.

A Brief Discussion of the Design Format of the Experiential Section

You have explored a number of examples of the experiential section. In addition, you have a definitional framework for the critical and variable attributes of the experience and its relationship to the debriefing section. You also have a list of materials for the learners and leaders. All of these add up to a relatively comprehensive picture of the design format for the experiential section.

Within limits, the experiential section may be in the form of different instructional design formats. For example, it may be an instructional simulation game, a Rolemap, or a piece of Learner Controlled Instruction. For more detailed information on the format of these different designs, you may refer to the other books in *The Instructional Design Library.*

A Longer Discussion of the Design Format of the Debriefing Section

Debriefing is a very critical component of an experiential learning package. You have the same number of examples and the same types of conceptual frameworks for this section as you do for the experiential section. However, only a limited number of other reference materials are available on debriefing. Therefore, we are about to undertake a fairly lengthy discussion on this topic below. As you read the following material, based on a series of articles which appeared in *SIMAGES* (Spelvin, 1979), remember that they are written for the *leader* of experiential learning packages rather than for the designer. However, you will find the procedural model presented in this chapter to be useful in designing your debriefing section.

The model divides the debriefing activity into two major phases: The first phase clears the air by providing an opportunity for learners to express their emotions in a nonjudgmental environment. The second phase facilitates a systematic and objective analysis of the experience.

Handling Emotions in Debriefing

"The purpose of debriefing is to help people to rationally reflect on their experience and to derive useful generalizations from it."

"The first step in debriefing is to encourage people to express their feelings without any attempt at analyzing them."

The second statement appears to contradict the first, but this is not true. The best way I can explain my point is by sharing an experience I had when I first tried out an adaptation of Paul Twelker's end-of-the-world simulation.

This is what happened: We lock up six people in a small bathroom and seal the door with masking tape. We play an audiotape recording which is presumably the voice printout of a doomsday computer. The voice tells the group that they are the only survivors on earth after a nuclear holocaust. From time to time, it instructs the group to discuss such long-term issues as how to perpetuate humankind and such short-term ones as whether to let in someone else (who is knocking at the door) and run the risk of killing everyone

through radiation. After about 45 minutes of critical incidents and controversial debates, the computer reports an
accident in the life-support system, declares that the survivors
are also going to die soon, and goes out of action with a
groan.

We open the doors to let the people out. I am ready with
my debriefing questions on factors that influence the
behavior of small groups under stress. But even to a
task-oriented, rational behaviorist like me, it is obvious that
the two sobbing people and the other four with their stunned
looks are in no shape to hold a calm, intellectual discussion
of the topic.

Many people concede that some kind of emotional
catharsis is necessary after an intense experience and before
an objective analysis. But they argue that most of their
mundane instructional experiences involve very little feelings
and therefore require no emotional release. This may be true,
but it is difficult to put yourself in a participant's place and
decide whether affective debriefing is required or not. Most
experiential learning activities contain elements of conflict
(against chance, time limits, performance standards, or other
players) and constraints (through external rules and limited
resources). These factors create feelings of frustration,
hostility, and futility. So, why take a chance? Why not clear
the air with a brief and simple cathartic session before
settling down to analyzing the experiential data and inferring
general principles?

Learning the Skills

Trainers and game leaders frequently skip the affective
debriefing activity because they feel that they do not have
sufficient skills for dealing with human emotions. Worse than
an inept handling of human emotions is the act of totally
ignoring them. It is perhaps better to face an emotional
outburst rather than to convert it into smoldering resent-

ment or nameless anxiety. If you are afraid to dabble with emotions, the step to skip is not debriefing but the experiential activity in the first place.

The skills of handling emotions and feelings are learnable skills. These skills and the knowledge base are simple to understand; they are *not* simple to implement, due to your own feelings and emotions. With practice, however, you should be able to gain competence and confidence in this area. A simple shaping procedure which I found useful in my own training is to begin with fairly neutral cognitive activities and gradually move into more and more affective ones. The basic skills needed for your practice may be picked up by observing experienced debriefers or by reading books on structured experiences (e.g., Pfeiffer and Jones, 1976), interpersonal communication (e.g., Becvar, 1974), or counseling (e.g., Vriend and Dyer, 1974).

What You Do *NOT* Have to Do

Debriefing is not psychoanalysis. Dealing with emotions is not the same as providing therapy. Its purpose is merely to facilitate people's expression of emotions—both positive and negative—so that they can settle down for an objective analysis of what they have experienced. A simple focus on this purpose should relieve you of unnecessary anxiety. Remember that you do not have to solve someone's sadness or answer anyone's anger. You do not have to analyze, understand, or explain any emotion at this time. You merely permit expression of emotions and protect people's rights to do so. You do this by listening attentively, empathically, and nonjudgmentally.

The one important rule for this phase of debriefing is that no one is required to express anything unless he or she wants to. As the leader of the group, it is your task to protect the privacy of people who need it. Avoid an obsessive need to be a psychic Peeping-Tom and discourage all peer pressure.

Explain at the beginning of this activity that participation is entirely optional. Remind people of this fact whenever necessary.

How to Begin

A simple technique for eliciting emotional expressions is to ask for it. Say something like, "Before we get into a systematic analysis of the activity, let's check out our feelings. During the activity, you might have experienced some strong feelings, such as anger, joy, sadness, or intimacy. If any of you would like to share your feelings with others, you are welcome to do so. But you don't have to, if you don't want to." That should be sufficient: No further elaborations or explanations are necessary.

Unless you are dealing with an experienced group which has done this kind of thing before, you may not find any eager volunteers. The ensuing silence could be very disquieting to you, and you may feel a need to fill it rapidly with empty talk. But stop for a moment to remind yourself that there is nothing dangerous about silence and that people may learn even when no one is talking. Try to figure out the reason for any silence before you intervene:

• Perhaps people are thinking and trying to get in touch with their feelings. (Actually, it may even be a good idea to request a couple of minutes of silence to help people look inwardly.) You may want to suggest that if people find the others distracting, they may retire to a corner or close their eyes. You may also try incomplete sentences, such as "During the game I felt . . ." and "Right now, I feel . . . ."

• Perhaps people are attempting to find words to express what they feel and are having problems because traditional education does not train students in this area. During the first few sessions, you may find it useful to provide a checklist or thesaurus of emotional expressions.

• Perhaps people are unsure of how others would react to

their statements. If you suspect this is what is happening, make a statement yourself—about some feeling you may have at this time. Do not create an artificial example, and be sure that your statement is related to the common experience.

In any case, after a suitable period of silence, if nothing happens, you may want to prompt the group with some models. Here are two suggested techniques:

Report any emotional action you might have observed during the earlier activity (e.g., one player always standing aloof) or any remark you might have overheard (e.g., "Let's fix those crooks when our team gets a chance to be the police!"). You do not have to name names in this process.

Provide samples from previous debriefing sessions.

In either of these cases, do not supply too many examples of the same type. Mix positive and negative emotional statements: anger, joy, sadness, and enjoyment.

Listen

Once the participants loosen up and start expressing their emotions, your job is mainly to model good listening behaviors. Based on Becvar's (1974) book, here are some suggestions:

- *Listen attentively.* Look directly at the speaker. Listen to both the content and the feeling of what is being said. Hear what the speaker is saying and also attend to other cues, such as the posture, facial expression, gestures, and tone.
- *Listen empathically.* Nonverbally invite the speaker to continue talking. Behave in a manner which is consistent with the expressed feelings. Mirror the emotions.

When and How to Intervene

While for the most part the best thing for you to do is to keep your mouth shut, you may have to intervene in some special cases:

- Remember that this phase of debriefing is for expressing

one's emotions. If the speaker begins to *analyze* his or her (or other people's) feelings or to intellectualize about the earlier activity, stop him or her politely. Remind everyone that there is another phase to debriefing which permits people to explore the "why's" of these emotions.

• Sometimes you may not understand the speaker's statement. Or, you may receive contradictory verbal and nonverbal messages, as in the case of a participant reporting that she is raging mad but in very cool, controlled tones. In these cases, you ask for clarification, but before you do so, make sure that you are not expressing a judgment or entrapping the speaker. Also, it is possible that a person has ambivalent feelings toward something, and he or she is expressing that through apparently contradictory statements. When you ask for clarification, clearly indicate what it is that you do not understand.

• Sometimes the speaker may create confusion by attempting to be indirect in the expression of his or her emotions. Help out the speaker by offering your guess of what he or she is trying to say and by requesting more direct expression.

• Sometimes the speaker may attack another person. This presents a dilemma for you, since you have to give the speaker sufficient space to express his or her emotions, and you also have to protect the other person's rights. Suggest that the speaker limit his or her statements to feelings rather than attempting to find their causes. If the other person counter-attacks, firmly stop the exchange and suggest that they discuss their grievances at a later time.

In Case of Emergencies . . .

From time to time, you may be confronted with some emotional outbursts following an experiential activity. Here are some guidelines for what to do in these situations:

• The first rule is to keep your cool and remind yourself

that *you* are not the target, generally (but see below). The emotional outburst does not indicate failure on your part. If the other participants become embarrassed, it is their problem. Actually, such outbursts may provide a growthful experience for everyone.

• A very useful approach to any type of debriefing, and especially in this affective phase, is the use of dual facilitators. When a co-facilitator is available, one of you can pay individual attention to the emotional person, while the other continues with the rest of the group. You may take the emotional participant to another room or to a corner and listen to his or her statements.

• If you do not have a co-facilitator, you may suggest that the troubled person retreat to a safety zone and be alone for a while. You may also tell the participant that you would like to discuss his or her feelings at a later time on an individual basis. Make sure that if you make this statement, you follow it up.

When You Are the Target

One of the occupational hazards of being a game leader of experiential activities is participants' use of you as a scapegoat for their frustrations. It is hard for you to keep calm while being subjected to an angry outburst. Suggest to the angry participant that to save other people's time, you would like to meet him or her individually after the session.

Keeping the Ball Rolling

Discourage any attempt to monopolize by a few vociferous participants. After a person has made an expression of his or her emotions, here are three suggested things for you to do:

• Paraphrase the statement without any deprecation of judgment. This signals the end of that speaker's turn and acknowledges that you have heard the message.

• Thank and reinforce the speaker for sharing his or her feelings with others.

• Move on to the next person who wants to speak or, if there is no one else, to the next activity.

On with the Debriefing

This affective phase of debriefing does not usually require too much time. This is just a preliminary activity designed to provide everyone a chance to let off some steam. You are now ready to proceed to the next phase of debriefing, in which you focus on a rational analysis of the content and the consequences of the experiential activity. Some of the expressions of emotions during this first phase may become useful data for examination during the second phase. However, it would be a good idea to separate these two sessions with a break in between.

Individual Sessions After Debriefing

Remember that you promised to meet with the troubled person after the session. Do so as soon as possible. The approach required to listen to an individual who is frustrated or depressed is very similar to that suggested earlier, except you need more patience and understanding. For further suggestions on facilitating interpersonal communication in these situations, check with books on counseling (e.g., Becvar, 1974).

After the session, you may also meet some angry participant who is *mad* at you. Here are some suggestions (based on Jones and Banet, 1976, and Ellis, 1977) for use during your confrontation:

• *Acknowledge and accept the message.* Do not ignore the situation or try to make light of the fact that the participant is angry about something you did or failed to do.

• *Acknowledge your own feelings.* Let the other person know that you are feeling defensive and that this may interfere with mutual communication.

• *Clarify the situation.* Usually, anger arises when there is a discrepancy between expectations and actual events. Find out what the other person's unmet expectations are and share your own expectations and assumptions.

• *Renegotiate the relationship.* Express regrets and exchange apologies. Plan for mutual avoidance of similar frustrations in the future. If an agreement is not possible, schedule another meeting after a cooling-off period, preferably with a mediator.

• *Implement your agreement.* Make sure that you are not holding any resentment and plotting to "punish" the other person later. Proceed with the task and help the other person to do the same.

Where Do You Go from Here?

The purpose of this section is to provide you with a beginner's tool kit for undertaking the affective component of debriefing. No claim is made for comprehensiveness, and no guarantee is given for infallibility. I have summarized the guidelines into a convenient checklist in Figure 3. Practice is necessary to put these principles in action. But practice alone will not guarantee learning. You need to debrief yourself after each experience before you become confident and comfortable. In general, you are not likely to encounter any negative emotional outbursts or intense anger. And even if you come across such an episode, I hope that you are able to convert it into a mutually growthful experience.

Directed Discovery in Debriefing

Experiential learning occurs not from the raw experience itself, but from objective reflection on its content and consequences. Systematic debriefing facilitates this kind of reflection. To maximize the effectiveness of debriefing, you, as the leader, have to maintain a delicate balance in two related domains:

• *Telling everything and covering up.* During the debriefing session, lecturing is ineffective and letting learners rediscover everything is inefficient. Insights presented by the leader are much less effectively learned than those which are actively derived by the learner and related to their experience. However, requiring a rediscovery of known laws in different disciplines by pondering on limited experiences consumes an enormous amount of time and results in frustration and dangerous half knowledge. In debriefing, you attempt to arrive at an ideal position between these two extremes.

• *Rigidity and sloppiness.* Structuring everything that takes place during debriefing does not facilitate innovative insights. A total laissez-faire approach, on the other hand, may not encourage the learners to focus on the task. In the debriefing procedure which we explore below, we suggest a balance by providing an overall structure and letting specific details take care of themselves.

Before You Begin

Before you move into this phase of debriefing, you should have done the following three things:

1. *List principles.* The experiential activity is designed to present some basic principles to the learners. Even before you assign this activity, you should have prepared a list of these principles, based on the goals of the activity and its model of reality. While the others are undergoing the experience, you may have an opportunity to observe them unobtrusively. For example, during a practice teaching session, you may note the statements and behaviors of different students. Based on this information, you may want to revise your original list of principles and rearrange them in order of their saliency during the experience. (Incidentally, this activity prevents you from interfering with the experiential section.)

2. *Determine exposure time.* During the experiential section, you might have undertaken some hidden moves to

Figure 3

Suggestions for Conducting Affective Debriefing

WHEN TO DO IT
- Do it immediately after the experiential activity, if possible.
- Do it even if you think that the earlier activity has not aroused any feelings.

WHAT TO FOCUS ON
- Remember that the purpose of affective debriefing is to give everyone an opportunity to express their current emotions.
- Remember that affective debriefing is *not* in-depth analysis or therapy.

HOW TO BEGIN
- Invite people to share their current emotions.
- Emphasize that this is a voluntary, optional activity. No one has to share if he or she does not want to.

HOW TO PROMPT
- Give some quiet time for people to think about what they feel.
- Provide a checklist of emotional expressions.
- Increase participants' trust by making an authentic emotional statement yourself.
- Provide sample statements from previous debriefings of the activity.

HOW TO LISTEN
- Listen attentively to the content and the feelings of the speaker.
- Listen empathically by reflecting the speaker's emotions.

HOW TO INTERVENE
- Discourage all attempts to analyze the emotions. Remind the speaker about the second phase to come later.
- Ask for clarification of statements you do not understand and statements that appear contradictory. Do so without appearing to trap the speaker.

(Continued on Next Page)

Figure 3 (Continued)

- Help the speaker to directly express his or her feelings.
- Discourage personal attacks. Suggest a focus on emotions instead of their causes.

HOW TO HANDLE OUTBURSTS
- Keep calm. Don't become defensive.
- Pay individual attention to the troubled person while your co-facilitator continues with the group.
- Suggest that the troubled person retire to be alone. Follow up with a meeting after the session.
- When a person gets angry at you, suggest an individual meeting.

HOW TO CLOSE
- Paraphrase the speaker's statement to indicate closure.
- Thank and reinforce the speaker for expressing his or her emotions.
- Proceed immediately to the next person or task.

HOW TO MOVE ON
- Keep this phase of debriefing short and proceed to the more reflective phase.
- Have a coffee-and-decompression break before the next phase.

HOW TO HANDLE PERSONAL ATTACKS
- Acknowledge the other person's anger and his or her right to be angry.
- Indicate your own defensiveness.
- Clarify the situation in terms of expectations and assumptions.
- Express regrets, exchange apologies, and renegotiate your relationship.

illustrate a point. For example, the blind person who appeared on the scene may not really be blind, or the "random" deal of cards could have been from a carefully stacked deck, or one team might have been given more poker chips than the others. It is very important that all learners have access to relevant information *at the end* of the debriefing session. But what information to reveal at what time during debriefing is a strategic question. You need to make a decision about the timing of your confessions so that their instructional value is maximized.

3. *Clear the air.* Rational reflection on a common experience and its objective analysis are facilitated if the participants are individually centered and jointly focused on the task. This state of readiness is difficult to achieve immediately after an intense experience when too many feelings and emotions are floating around in everyone's head. Before you launch into this rational phase of debriefing, you should have cleared the air by giving everyone an opportunity to express their feelings.

Orienting the Group

Let's assume that you have prepared yourself and your participants for this phase of debriefing. You begin by orienting the learners to the *content* and the *method* of what is going to happen.

Provide an advance organizer to the content by stating the objective for the experiential learning activity. You do not have to list all the specific behavioral objectives with their conditions and standards, but you should identify the general domain with such statements as the following:

- "The object of this project is to explore the dimensions of social concerns of a corporation in its advertising policy."
- "We are about to explore what it feels like to be a woman in a male-dominated organization and how it affects the performance of different people."

- "We want to explore how such factors as power, affluence, payoffs, and previous experiences affect the way different people form coalitions."

You may already have given your learners the goals and objectives of the experiential exercise at an earlier time. Even then, they should be reminded of these goals to focus their attention on the task at hand.

In orienting the learners to the method you want to use for this phase of debriefing, you emphasize the need for structure and flexibility. I usually make a brief statement such as this: "All of us went through an intense experience, and each of us has a lot of information and insights to share with the others. Unfortunately, all of us cannot talk about all things at the same time. In order to make sure that we share important elements of our experiences and infer some general principles by processing this information, I am going to structure our communication process during this session. Please make sure that your comments and reports are related to the topic under discussion at various times. I hope that this process is not too constraining. If some of your important thoughts have not been presented near the end of the session, you can ask for equal time during the open-ended segment which is scheduled later."

One Principle at a Time

You are now ready to direct the discovery of the basic principles from the experiential activity. We suggest a simple procedure which elicits these three items of information from the learners:

> Information related to a specific principle from their experiences.

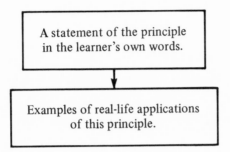

You repeat this process taking one principle at a time—both from your own list and from those suggested by your learners. In the end, you organize these principles in some meaningful fashion.

Figure 4 graphically presents the debriefing procedure. I will walk you through this chart to demonstrate its application. You may find the flowchart to be a handy summary and a performance aid during your debriefing sessions.

Asking Questions

Let's assume that you are ready to go to work. As the flowchart suggests, you begin with the first principle on your list and ask yourself whether the experiential activity generated enough data related to this principle. Since you have followed my earlier suggestion and arranged your list of principles in order of their saliency during the experience, your learners have sufficient data. Your next task is to ask a set of leading questions to help the learners discover this principle. Let's pretend that your learners participated in the simulation game, JOINT VENTURE. Let's also pretend that the principle you are trying to elicit goes something like this: "Players with fewer resources are more likely to initiate negotiations toward coalition formation." Your leading questions may include the following:

- "Think back about different rounds of the game. How many players had the card with a 5 during a round? . . . Did you go out looking for partners or did you wait for other players to come to you?"

- "How many players had the Ace during a round? . . . During that round, did you go out searching for partners or did you wait for other players to come to you?"
- "Which players had both 5 card and Ace card rounds? Think back and tell me how your coalition behavior changed in those two situations."

Your participants will be responding to each question before you proceed to the next one. Listen carefully to the response and summarize the information on the chalkboard or a flipchart.

Generating Principles

With this obvious example, your learners see the inverse relationship between the value of the card and the eagerness to seek coalitions. Some of them may spontaneously blurt out a statement of the principle. If this does not happen, you ask the learners if they can explain the relationship between the value of the card and the tendency to wait for partners. Summarize the principle and write it down on the chalkboard. Generally, an "if . . . then" structure is most effective. For example: *If* you have a higher card, *then* the less likely you are to go looking for partners.

Relating to Real Life

After you have successfully elicited a principle, you are ready to help your learners relate it to their real world. A simple way to do this is to say, "Can anyone give me a real-life example of this principle in action?" Hopefully, there will be some volunteers with such statements as the following:

- "When my dad started his business ten years ago, he went around to all the local businesses offering to do their bookkeeping. Now that his business has grown big and we have enough money, he doesn't have to

Figure 4

Debriefing Procedure for Eliciting Principles

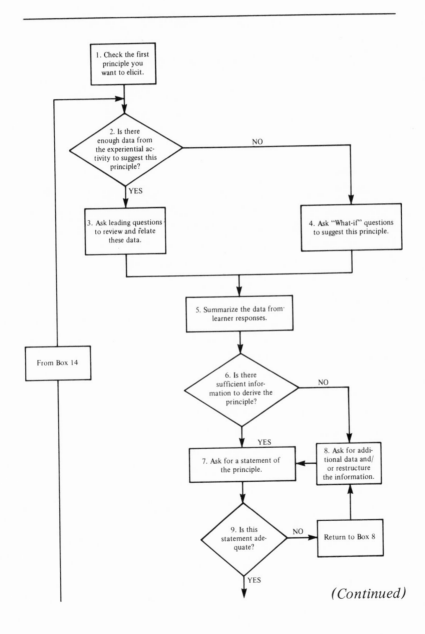

(Continued)

Figure 4 (Continued)

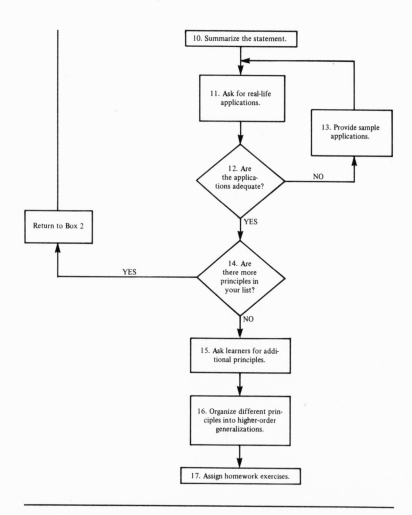

worry any more. He just sits down and waits for people to come and make a deal."

- "My kid has a model rocket club and when he wants to buy something and has no money, he goes to the other members asking them to chip in. But when he has some money saved up, he doesn't go for a joint purchase. He wants to save some more and buy the rocket all by himself so that he can do whatever he wants, whenever he wants."

Asking "What-If" Questions

Let's walk through the flowchart once again—this time with a pessimistic outlook. To begin with, learners do not have enough data related to the next principle. You were expecting that the play of the simulation game would follow a certain path, but it did not. In a situation like this, you might want to resort to a "what-if" question, such as the following: "What do you think would have happened, if all the players started out a round with exactly the same card?"

The "what-if" question is also useful when the players have some relevant data, but it does not point to the principle you are trying to elicit. This may happen in the following two cases:

1. The learners played an insufficient number of rounds and did not get enough data.
2. The learners played the bigger game of anticipating where you are leading them and sabotaging your moves.

Here are some examples of "what-if" questions being used in these situations:

- "What if we played the game for 200 rounds, and maintained the same level of interest! What do you think would have happened to this trend?"
- "What if 200 different teams played the game! If we asked all of them this question, how do you think their responses would be distributed?"

- "I sense that you were all too polite to each other and, after all, it was just play money. If this were real life and you were going after real profits, do you still think you would form a commune and split the money equally?"
- "I feel that you all conspired to mess up my beautiful plan. If you did not feel manipulated and if this were real business with real money, how would you behave in this situation?"

Brightening the Process

Let's assume that you have elicited all relevant data from the learners, but they are still unable to see the relationship among various factors. In this situation, we resort to Douglas Ellson's brightening process of providing more and more clues and gradually simplifying the inferential task until we reach the level at which the learners can "discover" the principle. Here are some of the things you can do:

- You can rearrange the data in a tabular form:

	High card (5)	Low card (A)
Look for a partner	4	17
Wait for a partner	15	2

- You can use a graphical form like this:

- You can break a complex principle into simpler ones:

"What happens when your offer to become a partner is turned down by the other team? Would you feel inclined to form a coalition with that team during a future round?"

"Let's assume that the other team treated you nicely and gave you an equal share in the profit, even though your contribution to the general fund was just one third. Would you feel inclined to team up with these people during a future round?"

- You can identify the variables clearly:

"We are trying to relate your experiences in previous rounds to your behavior in future rounds. We are trying to see if there is any rejection by a team during the second round and your response to their overtures during the third one."

- Finally, you can provide your learners with a multiple-choice decision:

"When you are repeatedly rejected by another team, do you feel that you will be more inclined to reject or accept this team's offers in a future round?"

It is very unlikely that you would have to go through the entire sequence to elicit a principle during debriefing. If this happens, you may want to return to the experiential section and make suitable modifications.

If you run into difficulties in transferring principles to real-life applications, you may provide some samples. You should be able to think up these samples from your own life or from some piece of fiction, history, or even a television series. Make a note of especially meaningful examples from your learners. You may want to use these anecdotes as prompts for other groups.

Getting Closure

Let's assume that you have exhausted your list of principles. Before you conclude this phase of the debriefing, however, here are three more things for you to do:

Elicit learner-discovered principles. Review the list of

principles and ask the participants if they can think of any more. Listen to each principle and write it down on the chalkboard. Do not become upset if you did not think of it first, or if the principle contradicts what you believe. Instead of passing judgment on its validity, process it through the same procedure (of recalling relevant data, deriving the principle, and finding real-life applications). Let your learners reject, revise, or recommend the principle on the basis of this procedure.

Organize the principles. You are now ready to organize different principles into higher-order generalizations. Here are three different ways to do this:

- Make up a matrix of possible "causes" and "results" and indicate their relationships.
- Take your "if . . . then" statements of principles and increase the number of factors on both sides of your set-up.
- Assume an increase in one factor and track down all of its direct and indirect consequences in the ensuing chain reaction.

Follow up assignments. Some of the higher-order organizations of the principles may be assigned to individual learners or to small groups as homework assignments. Other types of assignments include the following:

- Reading research articles and relating them to the experience.
- Collecting more examples of real-life applications through observation and interviews.
- Designing and conducting experiments to explore some of the variables in greater detail.
- Brainstorming applications of various principles.
- Writing a paper which summarizes the principles and supports them with research data.
- Redesigning the experiential section to make specific principles more salient.

A Concluding Caveat

Our approach to debriefing may make many people uncomfortable with its tight structure. They claim that engineering insights and directing discoveries are intrinsically incompatible procedures. However, my own experiences in using this approach and observing others use it suggest that the procedure provides the needed organization that is sorely lacking in most debriefing sessions. As long as this procedure is used as only one of the elements in the total debriefing process and is complemented by more affective and free-flowing activities, it seems to increase the effectiveness and efficiency of experiential learning.

Summary

Experiential learning packages contain materials that give instructions and information. These materials may be designed for the learners and/or the leaders of the activity. They structure both the experience and the debriefing.

The design of experiential learning materials may be analyzed in terms of such packaging considerations as size and media usage. Other variable dimensions include the type and level of specificity of the instructional goal and the relationship between the experience and the debriefing (in terms of their relative proportion, time lag between the two, and the dispersion of debriefing sections). The experience part of the package may be analyzed in terms of its level of simulation and of dissimulation, tightness of structure, learner role and interaction, and leader's role. Similarly, the debriefing part may be analyzed in terms of degree of structure, learner role and interaction, and leader's role.

The experience part may appear in a variety of instructional design formats. The debriefing part is usually divided into two phases. The first one clears the air and the second clarifies various principles. This chapter provided practical guidelines for maintaining the focus of the affective debriefing, initiating and facilitating free expression of feelings, intervening during major outbursts and personal attacks, and concluding this phase. The chapter also provided a systematic procedure for asking leading questions to focus the learner's attention on the experiential data related to a specific principle, eliciting a statement of the principle, relating it to real-life examples, and combining it with other principles to obtain higher-order generalizations.

References

Becvar, R.J. *Skills for Effective Communication: A Guide to Building Relationships.* New York: John Wiley and Sons, 1974.

Ellis, A. *How to Live with—and Without—Anger.* New York: Thomas Y. Crowell Company, 1977.

Jones, J.E., and A.G. Banet. Dealing with Anger. In J.W. Pfeiffer and J.E. Jones (Eds.), *The 1976 Annual Handbook for Group Facilitators.* La Jolla, California: University Associates, 1976.

Pfeiffer, J.W., and J.E. Jones. *The 1976 Annual Handbook for Group Facilitators.* La Jolla, California: University Associates, 1976.

Spelvin, G. Handling Emotions During Debriefing. *SIMAGES,* 1979, *1*(1).

Spelvin, G. Directed Discovery in Debriefing. *SIMAGES,* 1979, *1*(2).

Vriend, J., and W.W. Dyer. (Eds.) *Counseling Effectively in Groups.* Englewood Cliffs, New Jersey: Educational Technology Publications, 1974.

IV.

OUTCOMES

This chapter deals with the results of using experiential learning packages in training and education. Our interaction in the earlier pages is based on a shared belief in the effectiveness of this instructional design format. However, I do not want this chapter to become a testimonial to the power of these packages. This is not due to any scholarly modesty but to the fact that behind every positive outcome, there lurks a negative hazard. Any excessive emphasis of the former only leads to eventual disillusionment.

This chapter is divided into seven major areas related to the use of learning packages:

(1) confidence in learning;
(2) recall of what has been learned;
(3) transfer of skills;
(4) reality shock;
(5) affective effects;
(6) reactions of others; and
(7) preparation for life-long learning.

In each of these areas, I have juxtaposed positive and negative outcomes to emphasize that they are the sides of the same coin. The statements about these outcomes are based on my personal experiences and not on any experiential data. They suggest some guidelines to practitioners rather than topics to theoreticians.

1. Experiential Learning Packages Provide Greater Confidence in What Has Been Learned, . . .

"I didn't know I had it in me until I did the experiment."

At the end of some of my workshops, after a brief posttest, I ask participants to rate their level of confidence in what they have learned. A workshop which involves very few experiential elements usually results in a low confidence level, even though the posttest scores are high. In contrast, an experiential learning workshop may not result in high posttest scores, but the learners are much more confident about what they have learned. One of the major positive outcomes of experiential learning is this type of confidence, especially in one's psychomotor skills and affective abilities. A person may carefully study a driver's manual or listen to a lecture on public speaking, but until he or she undertakes at least a short experiential exercise, there is very little feeling of mastery. All people gain confidence from experiential learning, and to some people it is the only way to prove their competencies to themselves. Without the experience, they feel fraudulent about their claims to knowledge.

. . . but Learners Seem to Lack a Sense of Learning.

"No, Mom, we didn't learn anything in school today. We just played UNITED NATIONS all day long."

If you check with a learner in the midst of an experiential learning episode, it is very likely that he or she is unaware of any learning taking place. One reason for this is the way people associate learning with *verbal and factual information* and not with *intuitive insights.* Another reason is that the learner is so engrossed in the experience that the incidental learning becomes transparent. This lack of "feeling" of learning is one of the major problems with experiential learning materials. This is a major reason for the debriefing session, during which you point out to the learners that they *have* learned something and provide useful labels to think and talk about what they have learned.

2. Experiential Learning Is More Resistive to Forgetting, . . .

"The only things I remember from my fifth grade are the symbols we used in mapping our neighborhood."

A major positive outcome of learning from an experiential package is the long-term memory for what you have learned (in contrast to learning from books and lectures, which you forget the day after the final examination). Right now, if you list a number of things you learned in your school days, it is very likely that the majority of the items involved some experience beyond passive reception. The reason for this strong memory is obvious: experiential learning provides more application, more meaningful association, and more repetition. It uses more different senses and more of everything else a memory book would recommend. And even if you forget some of your experiential learning, the time required for relearning it tends to be very short—especially if you return to the experiential materials.

. . . but You May Remember the Wrong Things.

"I could never forget the day I tripped and fell down during the class play."

What the learner receives during an experiential episode can seldom be as tightly controlled as in a textbook or a filmstrip. One of the negative consequences of this is a probability of some dramatic—but irrelevant—event becoming memorable. Much worse, this event could become so salient that it distracts the learner's attention from critical principles and procedures. The learner could not recall these important elements because he or she did not attend to them in the first place. For example, when I ask my son what he remembers learning from a simulation game which we played a year ago, he replies, "Always check to see if you have enough poker chips before you begin the game." All of the other cognitive principles about (and affective beliefs against) life in a police state, which the game was designed to teach, have been relegated to a secondary place in his frustrating pursuit of additional poker chips in the midst of the game.

3. Experiential Learning Packages Facilitate Transfer of Skills, . . .

"No problem. I've done this many times."

One criterion for effective learning is its applicability to real-life situations. Conventional classroom teaching does not transfer easily to problem situations. In contrast, one major positive outcome of learning through experience is the bridging of the gap between training and application. Experiential packages incorporate the outside world in a real or simulated form. They require application of principles and procedures to solve real problems. They provide realistic feedback. As a result, the learner is ready for his or her real-world job. Although the job requirements may differ from what he or she experienced during the training, these differences are significantly fewer when you compare them to the conventional academic education.

. . . but There Are Fewer Skills to Transfer.

"I know I use the same technique over and over again, but that's the only thing I know."

Experiential learning packages trade off breadth of coverage for depth of learning. In a lecture session, you can survey an enormous number of skills in a given field. During the same period of time, you can *experience* only a few of these skills in any detail. The result of this inefficiency is the limited set of alternatives available to the experiential learner. This is a serious problem for those who would like all learning to come through experience. The obvious way to reduce the impact of this problem is to combine a systematic verbal survey of a field with an in-depth experiential exploration of selected areas.

4. Experiential Learning Packages Reduce Disillusionment on the Job, . . .

"But my teacher never told me anything about that!"

I remember my first day as a teacher in a real-world classroom after ten months of learning how to teach English as a second language. Within the first 30 minutes, at least ten different crises arose, and I was totally unprepared for coping with any of them. None of my academic preparation helped me at that time. And that was only the first of the many occasions when I felt cheated by my textbook-lecture learning. In contrast, I remember my first journalistic assignment to interview a local politician. During the training course, I had gone through an experiential learning package which included playing the role of a reporter interviewing a tough and famous personality. I felt ready for the job assignment and even found it *easier* than the earlier role play.

This reduction of "reality shock" is one of the major outcomes of learning through an experiential package. The abrupt crash into the job world from the training environment is softened by this type of learning.

. . . but They Disappoint the Learner During the Learning Process.

"I give up. I'm ready to drop out!"

Experiential learning packages do not magically remove harsh aspects of reality; they merely introduce them earlier in the learning process. This may result in some motivational problems. For example, the usual approach to inservice training of regular teachers who are about to receive "mainstreamed" mildly handicapped children from special classes is to provide them with reassuring verbal training. (Later, when the teacher is faced with real mainstreamed children, he or she is shocked by the enormity of the problems.) One of our experiential packages in this area involves realistic case materials; this results in very early disillusionment and immediate resistance toward mainstreaming. It is very difficult to motivate the anxious teachers and have them focus on the relevant concepts and skills.

5. Experiential Learning Packages Are Very Effective for Affective Learning, . . .

"I know what it feels like to be an old person in a nursing home. I can feel the despair and loneliness in my guts."

You can analyze a feeling with words and approach it with visual media. But you can really acquire the feeling only by experiencing it. Some of the most powerful outcomes of learning from experiential packages are feelings, attitudes, and beliefs. For example, I have read a lot—both in fiction and nonfiction—about the evils of the caste system in India, and I have been moved by sensitive movies on the subject. But nothing changed my attitudes and shook up my beliefs as much as three days of living with an "untouchable" family during a social-service training program. This experience did not permit me the luxury of being an outside observer, but required me to function within the sociological constraints of living in a slum. Similar dramatic shifts in attitudes and values have been reported when trainees have been sent to "prisons" or have been required to restructure their lives on a facist model.

. . . but This Raises a Number of Ethical Issues.

"But this is brain-washing!"

In contrast to the neutral stance of the value clarification format (Kirschenbaum and Simon, 1973), you take a position before you design an experiential learning package. And in contrast to the openness of other types of experiential learning, where the learner picks and chooses elements of the outside world to construct his or her reality, you organize and structure your package to channel the learner's experience. This presents a powerful tool *and* a moral dilemma. This ethical issue has acquired some prominence in recent simulation gaming literature, where consumers are becoming increasingly conscious that one person's clarity of simulation could be another person's bias. An extremely negative outcome of experiential packages could be learners walking around with biased beliefs—even if they happen to be yours.

6. Experiential Learning Packages Bring Praise to the Users, . . .

"She's our most outstanding trainer . . . And that's because she doesn't do any of the usual training stuff."

One of the rewards for the trainer who uses experiential learning packages is support and reinforcement from others. Outsiders and administrators perceive the face validity of these packages, and the trainer's credibility goes up. Other trainers appreciate the risks involved in trying out an innovation in the traditional training situation and admire the person who could do it. Most importantly, learners appreciate the use of experiential learning packages and the freedom to learn on their own. Even if they do not thank the trainer, the change in their motivation is easy to see. As a result, the trainer grows in self-confidence and becomes eager to experiment with more innovative techniques.

. . . but They May Also Be Condemned by Others.

"Only trainers who are too lazy to prepare their lesson plans or who want to entertain their students use this fun-and-games stuff."

Unfortunately, the same trainer could be criticized for the use of the experiential package. Outsiders perceive it as a frivolous activity. Pop psychologists warn them against the dangers of these "heavy" approaches. Administrators judge the trainer's worth in terms of time spent in *lecturing* the class. They correlate noise and activity with lack of control. Other trainers classify experiential learning packages as radical departures from established routine. Worst of all, learners transfer their interpersonal problems and experiential frustrations to the trainer as the most convenient scapegoat. Unfortunately, these negative outcomes of using experiential learning packages are much more prevalent than the positive picture painted above.

7. Experiential Learning Packages Prepare Learners for Life-Long Learning, . . .

"I learn from ALL my experience."

Even those trainers and teachers who prepare their students to learn *throughout* life frequently forget to prepare them to learn *from* life. Training to become an independent learner usually focuses on how to use the library, how to read selectively, and how to take lecture notes. All of these skills deal with learning from formal, verbal, organized knowledge. To learn from life, you need skills that are acquired from experiential learning. A single experience with a learning package does not guarantee these skills, but repeated exposure results in the incidental learning of how to learn from all experiences. The learner learns to debrief himself or herself after every growthful experience. He or she becomes more aware of feelings and more able to express them. He or she also learns to center himself or herself and to calmly analyze the contents of the experience and of its consequences in order to learn personally meaningful lessons from it.

. . . but They Produce a Cynical Attitude Toward Formal Education.

"You can't believe ANYTHING you read."

An unfortunate consequence of learning from experiential packages is an increasing disbelief in conventional education and training. This disbelief becomes stronger as the learner acquires more skills through experiential learning and confronts more academically elegant, but totally trivial theory.

In most cases, this cynicism toward the printed page and the spoken word is justifiable. However, it would be a tragedy if it resulted in an over-generalized condemnation of all conventional education.

I hope that the juxtaposition of the positive and negative suggests some guidelines for accentuating the former and ·reducing the latter. Let's re-emphasize a recurring theme: Experiential learning packages are *not* for all learners, all topics, and all times. We should remember—and remind our consumers—that the exclusive use of experiential packages is an inefficient approach to learning.

Reference

Kirschenbaum, H., and S.B. Simon. *Readings in Value Clarification.* Minneapolis: Winston Press, 1973.

V.

DEVELOPMENTAL GUIDE

The examples and explanations in the preceding pages are designed to give you an understanding of the nature and use of experiential learning packages. In the following pages, we are ready to discuss the practical question of "How do we develop an experiential learning package?" This chapter presents a step-by-step procedure for the production of these packages, based on the "systems-approach" model to instructional development.

Before we present the model, I would like to present two caveats:

1. The design and development of an experiential learning package is a dynamic, interactive process; the model itself is a static, linear one. As you apply the model, feel free to skip a step and return to it later. Or, work simultaneously on different steps of the model. Use the model as a flexible set of guidelines rather than rigid requirements. But, at the same time, make sure that you are not disregarding the systematic procedure as an excuse for sloppy thinking.

2. Not all steps of the model are of equal importance. Nor do they all require the same amounts of time and effort. Depending upon your topic and situation, you may discard some of the steps and add others. After the description of the preferred model, I provide you with two alternative versions. You may find these more suited to your task and temperament.

The Three Major Stages of the Model

Figure 5 presents the three major stages of the model. Here are brief descriptions of each stage:

Analysis and prescription. You begin this stage with a fuzzy feeling that an experiential learning package could fulfill some of your instructional needs. During this stage, you systematically identify who your learners are, under what conditions they are going to use your package, and what cognitive and affective goals you would like them to achieve. At the end of this stage, you would have specified your package requirements and instructional objectives.

Design and development. You begin this stage with the specifications from the previous one. You then select appropriate formats (e.g., self-instruction, work with a partner, and small-group activity) and media (e.g., printed materials, audiotape, videotape) for your experiential and debriefing activities. The next step is to write and produce materials for use by *learners* and their *leaders.* The final step in this stage is to assemble and integrate different sections and components. At the end of this stage, you would have produced a prototype package.

Verification and revision. You begin this stage with your prototype package and improve its motivational effectiveness by repeatedly revising it on the basis of feedback from different experts, representative learners, and selected leaders. The final step in this stage is to conduct a summative field test which enables you to objectively measure and report the effectiveness of your package. At the end of this step, you would have created the "final" version of the package and obtained objective data on its effectiveness.

In the model, I am ignoring the important stage of diffusion and implementation. Through the application of this model, you may end up with an excellent package which is based on a thorough analysis and which has been systematically developed and effectively evaluated. However,

Figure 5

*Stages in the Development of an
Experiential Learning Package*

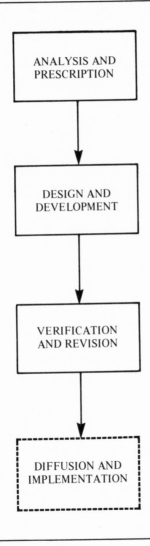

the package may fail in the hands of its users, if you do not pay attention to its implementation. Other than pointing this out and recommending an excellent book by Havelock (1973), I bypass this topic because it falls beyond the scope of this book.

Each stage of the model can be divided into a number of convenient steps. In the following pages, I shall outline these steps and provide you with a set of practical guidelines.

Steps in the Analysis and Prescription Stage

As you can see in Figure 6, the analysis and prescription stage consists of six different steps. Guidelines for each of these steps are given below:

Learner analysis. You begin this analysis by clearly identifying your target learners. Then you specify the characteristics of the learners which will help or hinder the use of the experiential learning package that you plan to develop. You do this directly by interviewing a few learners and by giving questionnaires and tests to others. You also do this indirectly by talking to teachers, trainers, and administrators. Remember that you are not conducting a sociological survey or an anthropological expedition. The types of information you collect should answer questions that are useful in the design of your package. Here are some samples:

- *What related background experiences do your learners already have?*
- *What skills and knowledge do the learners have in this area?*
- *What major misconceptions and prejudices are the learners likely to have?*
- *What is the attitude of the learners toward the content of your package?*
- *What is the attitude of your learners toward experiential learning as a technique?*

Figure 6

Steps in the Analysis and Prescription Stage

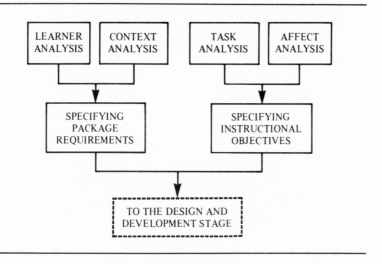

* *What media, language, and learning strategies do your learners prefer?*

Context analysis. It is not enough if you know all about your learners. You have to identify the situation in which they are going to learn from your package. You begin your context analysis by specifying this situation. Then you identify the factors which are likely to influence the use of your packages. You do this by interviewing people and by observing what happens during a typical instructional session. The types of questions for which you are attempting to find answers include the following:

* *Who are the instructors? What are their experiences, competencies, and preferences?*
* *How is the package going to be introduced into the existing program?*

- *What support facilities are available? What facilities are lacking?*
- *What media equipment is available?*
- *What types of physical space and furniture are available?*
- *What are the cost constraints? How much money can the system afford for the development of your packages? How much money can you spend on expendable materials?*
- *What are the scheduling constraints? How long can your experience and debriefing take?*

You may have different types of learners and different situations in which they use your packages. Therefore, it may not be possible for you to have single, clear-cut answers to each of these questions. Usually, you should identify both the "average" value and the range of the values.

Specifying package requirements. This step converts your learner and context analyses into a set of specifications for your experiential learning package. During this step, you may want to share the information with your colleagues and obtain their inputs in coming up with such specifications as the following:

- **Cost restrictions.** *What is the maximum budget for the development of the package? How much should each package cost? How much should the materials for each learner cost?*
- **Time restrictions.** *How much teacher/trainer time is available? How much learner time is available? How long can the entire exercise last?*
- **Resource constraints.** *What are the limits of physical space and furniture?*
- **Media constraints.** *What presentation media (e.g., videotape, filmstrip, etc.) can you not use because of*

*lack of equipment or because of the negative atti-
tudes of teachers, trainers, and learners?*
- **Role of leaders.** *What can you expect from the
teacher or trainer without additional training?*
- **Support facilities.** *What support can you expect in
terms of equipment, space, and personnel?*
- **Implementation design.** *How is your package going to
be introduced into the existing program?*
- **Language restrictions.** *What level and style of language should you use? What words and concepts do
you have to teach before the experiential activity?*
- **Entry level.** *How can you ensure a smooth integration
of your learning experience and the learner's entry
level?*
- **Motivational factors.** *How can you increase any
existing interest and reduce resistance?*

Task analysis. In this step, you specify the cognitive
objectives for your proposed package. You begin this analysis
by stating (in general terms) what you want your learners to
be able to do upon completion of the experience and the
debriefing. You then list all the simpler tasks which are
required for this desired competency. You keep repeating
this step of identifying simpler tasks which are required for
performing the earlier ones. Information about the learner's
entry level (from the earlier step of learner analysis) should
suggest a suitable stopping place for this analysis.

Affect analysis. In this step, you specify the affective
objectives for your proposed package. You begin this analysis
by stating (in general terms) the types of attitudes, beliefs,
and values you want the learner to acquire as a result of going
through your experiential package. You then "operational-
ize" this affective goal by identifying a set of behavioral
indicators.

Here is a sample affective goal from a teacher who is

designing an experiential package for her students who are deaf and who do not like to wear their hearing aids: "The child appreciates the use of the hearing aid." Here are the behavioral indicators obtained through an analysis of this goal:

- *The child uses the hearing aid voluntarily for listening to radio, TV, and record player.*
- *The child keeps the hearing aid in good functional order.*
- *The child wears the hearing aid during all waking hours, both in public and in private situations.*
- *The child uses the hearing aid to monitor his or her own voice in talking to others.*

Specifying instructional objectives. This step converts your learner and context analyses into a set of specific training objectives for the experiential learning package. During this step, you convert your subtasks (from the task analysis) and the behavioral indicators (from the affect analysis) into statements of enabling objectives and arrange them in an appropriate sequence. Here is a checklist to help you in this process:

- **Sufficiency.** *Make sure that your enabling objectives add up to the major cognitive or affective goal. If you have left out any important subtasks or behavioral indicators, add them to your list.*
- **Necessity.** *Remove any objective which is not necessary for the achievement of your cognitive goal.*
- **Sequence.** *If there is a logical order for attaining your objectives, make sure that your list is arranged in this order.*
- **Specificity.** *Rewrite any objectives which provide too many trivial details or use too many fuzzy words.*

- *Behaviorality. Make sure that each objective specifies an observable learner performance (or a product that results from learner performance).*
- *Conditions. List any tools, equipment, and reference materials which the learner may or may not use in demonstrating his or her competency.*
- *Standards. Include a specification of the minimum criteria for acceptable learner performance (e.g., time limit, percentage of accuracy, etc.).*

The objectives you have derived from the systematic analyses should assist you in structuring appropriate experiences and debriefing activities. As planning tools, these objectives ensure relevance and quality control in your design. However, they should not be perceived as being rigidly set in concrete. During the actual design and evaluation of your package, keep an open mind. If you come across an efficient bypath or an unanticipated side-effect, pursue it to see if you can achieve more instructional gains with little additional effort. Make the maximum use of any serendipitous opportunity without using it as an excuse for sloppy planning.

Steps in the Design and Development Stage

This stage can be conveniently divided into two major phases related to the *experiential* section and the *debriefing* section. Obviously, these two sections have to be integrated with one another in order to obtain your prototype package; see Figure 7.

The design of the two sections are interrelated as indicated by the broken arrow in Figure 7. Both design activities proceed in a parallel fashion as shown in Figure 8.

Each step in this figure is briefly described below:

Format selection for the experiential section. The instructional objectives and package requirements which were

Figure 7

Phases of the Design and Development Stage

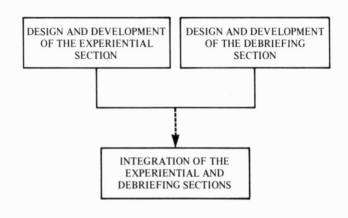

specified during the preceding analyses determine the format
for the experiential section. Alternative available formats
have been described and illustrated in the earlier sections.
Here are three sets of questions to help you in the selection
of a suitable format:

- *Should you use real-life or simulated experiences? If
  real-life, what is the probability that your learners
  have already experienced it? If simulated, what are
  the critical elements to be retained in your simulation? What information are you going to withhold
  from your learners?*
- *How tightly are you going to structure the experience?*
- *Do you want your learners to go through the
  experience individually or in small groups? Do you
  want them to work through the experience indepen-*

Figure 8

Steps of the Design and Development Stage

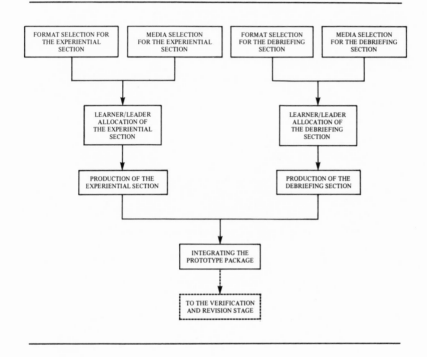

dently or collaboratively? If you are using small groups, do you want the members to have homogeneous or heterogeneous levels of knowledge, skills, and attitudes?

Media selection for the experiential section. You are now ready to select one or more suitable media (e.g., printed materials, audiotape, or videotape) to provide instructions for the experiential section. Here are some guidelines for media selection based on Stolovitch's (1978) recommendations:

- *Study your learner analysis information. Decide what types of media attributes (e.g., ease of use, color, portability, and referability) they need and prefer. Make a list of these attributes.*
- *Study your task analysis and affect analysis information. Decide what types of media attributes (e.g., motion, degree of realism, sound, and visual presentation) are required to achieve your instructional objectives. Make a list of these attributes.*
- *Study your context analysis information. Decide what type of media attributes (e.g., compatibility with available equipment, inexpensive materials, and adaptability) are needed in the situation in which your package is going to be used. Make a list of these attributes.*
- *Check your media production capabilities. Select the medium (or media combination) which has all the attributes you listed earlier.*

The key concept in Stolovitch's selection procedure is that you do not select a medium just because "everyone else" is using it or because of its aesthetic properties. Instead, you focus on what media attributes are required by your learners, the objectives, and the situation, and select the medium (or media combination) that can supply these attributes efficiently and effectively.

Learner/leader allocation of the experiential section. You are now ready to decide how the instructions for the experiential activity are to be divided between the learners and the leader. Your choice may range all the way from "leader-proof" materials which are directly presented to the learners (e.g., FABULOUS CHICKENS) to leader-mediated materials in which the learners become passive participants (e.g., STUPID STUDENTS). You may want to refer back to different examples in the previous chapters for suitable suggestions.

Production of the experiential section. This is the step in which you actually produce your experiential section based on your format and media selections and the allocations to learners and leaders. This step may involve writing for print, writing scripts, designing visuals, photography, recording, and other such activities. This is a major, time-consuming step. Because it may take a wide variety of forms, there are no general guidelines except to warn you against getting carried away from your instructional objectives into slick and cute media production under the illusion of artistic creativity.

Format selection for the debriefing section. The specific format for your debriefing will depend upon your analyses and upon the nature of your experiential section. Alternative formats have been described and illustrated in the earlier sections. Here are three questions to assist you in the selection of a suitable format:

- *How tightly do you want to structure your debriefing?*
- *Do you want your learners to be debriefed individually or in a group?*
- *Which type of learning do you want to emphasize: cognitive or affective?*

Media selection for the debriefing section. The usual alternatives range from a printed questionnaire to audiotape recordings. Selecting suitable media for the debriefing section is not likely to be as complex as in the case of the experiential section. However, you may want to use the same systematic procedure.

Learner/leader allocation of the debriefing section. The alternatives range from a self-debriefing questionnaire to a totally leader-controlled session. You may want to refer back to different samples in the earlier sections for suitable suggestions.

Production of the debriefing section. This is the step in which you actually produce your debriefing section based on your earlier decisions. Here are some guidelines based on the debriefing model described earlier:

- *Include a set of instructions to the leader on how to prepare for the debriefing session.*
- *Prepare some cathartic questions to clear the air immediately after the experiential activity. If a leader is to be involved, provide guidelines for handling this session.*
- *State the instructional objectives for use during debriefing. For the leader, provide a list of principles to be elicited during the second phase of debriefing. Also, provide guidelines to the leader on how to handle this session. If a leader is not to be involved, provide a set of questions and blank tables for recording the data so that a group can debrief itself.*

Integrating the prototype package. Many different components are produced during the design and development stage: the experiential and debriefing sections with different materials for learners and leaders. You may also have different mediated components, such as a videotape segment to introduce the experiential section, a set of printed instructions for the learners and leaders, and an audiotape for the debriefing section. Even if you are the only one involved in this production, it is very easy for you to lose track of all the bits and pieces. Before you rush into trying out your package, you need to sit down calmly and recheck that you have the materials assembled into an integrated package. Here are some guidelines for this step:

- *Make a list of materials and make sure that you have everything available in the right quantity and in the correct sequence. Imagine that you are a learner and work through the package to see if any essential component is missing. Do the same thing once again—this time imagining that you are the leader.*
- *Check for the accuracy of cross references. For example, if you require the learners to read an article, check its title and page number. Similarly, check for the accuracy of all references to the learner's guide.*
- *Check for consistency of language. In writing different sections at different times, you might have used different labels for the same concept.*
- *Check for continuity. Make sure that there are clear directions to move learners and leaders from one component to another. Make sure that these moves are as smooth as possible.*
- *Proofread all printed sections and check for the comprehensibility of media production. You do not need to test your materials with your learners to find obvious typographical errors or incomprehensible sound recordings.*
- *Get away from the materials for a couple of days and critically evaluate them with the help of your package specifications and instructional objectives. See if you could make some significant changes before proceeding to the next stage.*

Steps in the Verification and Revision Stage

This stage can be divided into two major phases: the formative phase for *improving* the effectiveness of the package and the summative phase for *proving* the effectiveness. Within the formative phase, there are the three steps of expert verification and revision, learner verification and revision, and total-package verification and revision. The different steps are illustrated in Figure 9 and briefly described below.

Expert verification and revision. The ultimate test of effectiveness of an experiential learning package is whether learners like it and learn from it. However, an experience which learners like very much, and from which they apparently learn a good deal, may teach totally inaccurate principles and undesirable attitudes. Hence, expert appraisal of an experiential package acts as a complementary check to learner performance data.

Different types of experts are qualified to pass judgment on various aspects of your package. A subject-matter specialist—a social psychologist, for example—helps to evaluate the appropriateness and adequacy of the instructional content by checking items such as the following:

- *Are the instructional objectives of this package compatible with the goals of social psychology?*
- *Does the experiential activity accurately reflect the realities of interpersonal interactions?*
- *Is the theoretical model acceptable to experts in the field?*

Another type of expert who may provide valuable feedback during this step is an instructional designer. This expert focuses his or her attention on the structure, the sequence of the experience, and the debriefing, and checks items such as the following:

Figure 9

Steps in the Verification and Revision Stage

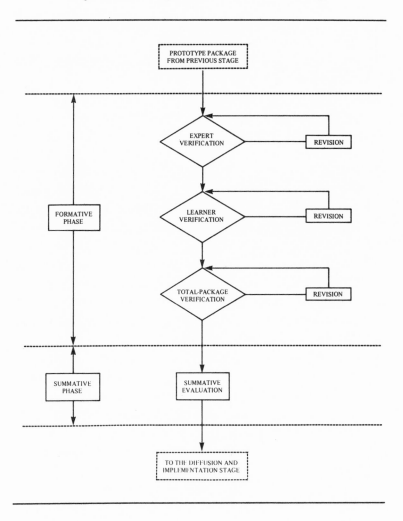

- *Is the learner subjected to any unnecessary risk during the experiential activity?*
- *Are the experiential episodes arranged in an effective sequence?*
- *Is the amount of chance in the simulation suitably controlled?*
- *Do the debriefing questions cover all basic principles?*

A third type of expert for this step is a trainer-administrator who is familiar with the learners and the situation in which your package is to be used. This expert will check the useability of the materials and methods by exploring these questions:

- *Can the experiential and debriefing activities be scheduled within the usual time constraints?*
- *Does the instructor require any special training to conduct the debriefing?*
- *Are the level and style of language suited to the learners?*
- *Will the learners find the package interesting?*

Here are some guidelines for maximizing the effectiveness of expert verification:

- *Identify more than one expert in each field. This will enable you to obtain more objective feedback.*
- *Use appropriate checklists to focus each expert's attention on his or her own field.*
- *In addition to your prototype package, provide relevant background information (about target learners, instructional context, and training objectives) to your experts.*

In making revisions on the basis of expert feedback,

remember that you cannot please all of the people all the time. Different parts of the feedback may contradict each other. You have to use your own judgment in deciding which revisions are likely to significantly improve the effectiveness of your package.

Learner verification and revision. You are now ready to try out your package on representative learners and revise it on the basis of their responses, reactions, and remarks. Here are some guidelines for this step:

- *Begin with a single person, unless your experience requires a group.*
- *Observe the experiential process and take notes on how it can be simplified and streamlined. Identify all unnecessary activities that do not contribute to the achievement of the goals. However, do not remove essential elements of reality.*
- *Make sure that the learners understand that you are not testing them—you are testing out the **material.** Encourage them to offer suggestions any time during the activity.*
- *Refrain from the temptation to "teach" the learners. Remember that you are merely observing their experiences and not coaching them from the sidelines.*
- *If your learners do not understand the instructions, and if this presents a major problem in the continuation of the activity, make suitable on-the-spot modifications. Write down these changes immediately.*
- *Have a colleague take copious notes during the debriefing session. Spend appropriate amounts of time during which you encourage your learners to suggest ways of improving the experiential package.*
- *Modify the materials immediately after the tryout. Repeat your tryout with a fresh group of learners.*

Continue this tryout-and-revision step until your package produces reliable results.

Total-package verification and revision. You are now ready to test the total package without participating in the experiential or debriefing process. In this step, you try out the package—both the learner's and the leader's materials—in a typical situation. Here are some guidelines for maximizing the effectiveness of this total-package verification:

- *Schedule a typical instructional session. For example, you may want to test your package as a part of an ongoing training session.*
- *Select a representative leader and give him or her the complete package. Refer the leader to the manual for all necessary instructions.*
- *Unobtrusively observe the leader's use of the package. From your earlier tryouts, you are familiar with the effects on the learners. Now focus your attention on what the leader is doing and what his or her problems appear to be.*
- *Observe the leader during the debriefing session. Take notes on the comments and responses from the learners.*
- *After the session, debrief the leader. Find out how he or she felt about the activity and ask for his or her opinions about the strengths and weaknesses of the package. Ask him or her for suggestions for improving the package.*
- *Compare the leader's use of the package with your use and identify major differences. Make suitable additions to incorporate those techniques which you use but have not included in the leader's materials.*
- *Make suitable revisions and repeat the total-package verification with another leader and another group of learners.*

Summative evaluation. This is the final field test to confirm the effectiveness of your package. Here are some suggestions for undertaking this step:

- *Construct (or collect) a wide variety of testing instruments to measure the achievement of your objectives. Similarly, construct (or collect) other instruments to measure related variables.*
- *To maintain a high degree of objectivity, have someone else undertake this final field test.*
- *Select a representative group of learners. Administer all pretest instruments to measure learners' knowledge, skills, and attitudes.*
- *Use the experiential learning package in as close a situation to its eventual use as possible.*
- *After the debriefing, measure learners' knowledge, skills, and attitudes, using the same instruments.*
- *Analyze the data and prepare a brief report on the learning gains.*

Alternative Approaches

The systems-approach model described above does not guarantee that you will end up with a creative and interesting package, but it does increase the probability of producing an effective one. Many people feel constrained about the extremely goal-oriented approach of this model and complain that it curbs their creativity. Although we have seen many creative people use this approach, if you do not like it (or if you want a change of pace), here are a couple of alternatives:

The Prima Donna Model. If you are a creative designer who needs to experiment, you may use the following approach:

1. Begin with a general idea of your instructional goal and forget all the analyses. Create an experiential activity using your intuition and ingenuity. Also, create an innovative debriefing session.

2. Get evaluative feedback from your colleagues and other experts only if you feel like it. Try out your package with a group of learners and make suitable changes. As long as you remain within the original, broad goal for the package, feel free to modify its specific objectives.

3. When your tryouts result in reliable learning, produce the final package. Identify the actual effects of the package and specify a list of instructional objectives based on them.

In addition to giving you more freedom, this approach has the following advantages:

• You produce your prototype package very early in the process. This saves time and resources and is especially helpful if you have a regular teaching or training assignment and cannot afford to undertake leisurely analyses.

• Any inaccurate assumptions you may make about your learners get corrected during the tryouts. Your final product reflects actual learner feedback rather than theoretical knowledge.

• The final package is the work of a single intellect rather than the creation of a committee. This provides internal consistency for the package and a sense of ownership to the developer.

• Because the prototype package is produced relatively rapidly, the developer does not become emotionally attached to it. Therefore, he or she is more likely to experiment with unexplored strategies.

The Better Mouse-Trap Model. Very often you come across a natural experience or a contrived activity which is highly motivating and provocative. When you feel that you have such a ready-made experience and would like to exploit it for its instructional value, you may want to use the following approach:

1. Try out the experience in different situations to see if you can produce reliable and useful results. Make minor changes in the activity during these tryouts.

2. If you are unable to produce the earlier results with a specific type of learner or in a particular situation, feel free to change the learners and the situation. Keep experimenting until you have identified the optimum users and conditions of use.

3. Let the learners report what they have learned in an open-ended fashion. Identify the insights and principles you want to emphasize and prepare debriefing questions to make them more salient.

4. When you are able to obtain reliable results, document your methodology for use by others. Also, analyze the actual effects and convert them into a set of instructional objectives.

This approach may appear to put the cart before the horse, but it does have a major advantage: You can use an existing, exciting experience without having to rediscover the wheel.

In either of these alternative approaches, the end results are the same as in the case of the original systems approach. You end up with an experiential learning package which has been verified and validated through learner testing. You also end up with a set of specific objectives which the package is able to achieve.

You now have three alternative approaches for your first development effort in this instructional design format. As long as you use the steps and stages of the model as flexible guidelines, you will find the design and development to be an exciting activity. Actually, the best way to learn to develop experiential learning packages is (as you might have guessed) through experience!

References

Havelock, R.G. *The Change Agent's Guide to Innovation in Education.* Englewood Cliffs, New Jersey: Educational Technology Publications, 1973.

Stolovitch, H.D. *Audiovisual Training Modules.* Englewood Cliffs, New Jersey: Educational Technology Publications, 1978.

VI.

RESOURCES

JOURNALS

Journal of Experiential Learning and Simulation. Published by Elsevier North Holland (52 Vanderbilt Avenue, New York, New York 10017).

This is a quarterly journal with the objectives of sharing current knowledge and understanding of experiential learning and simulations; advancing the theory, design, and techniques used in experiential learning and simulation; and promoting the use of these pedagogical approaches. Each issue contains articles focusing on the design of experiential/simulation exercises; research on the use of specific activities; descriptions of innovative experiential exercises/simulations; and projections on the future of the field.

SIMAGES. Published by the North American Simulation and Gaming Association (Treasurer, NASAGA, Box 100, Westminster College, New Wilmington, Pennsylvania 16142).

This journal maintains an informal tone, and through its regular departments keeps the reader informed about the latest events in the Association and in the field. In addition to ready-to-use experiential activities and games, each issue contains a number of practical articles related to the design and use of games and simulations and similar activities.

Simulations and Games. Published by SAGE Publications (275 South Beverly Drive, Beverly Hills, California 90912).

This quarterly journal provides an interdisciplinary forum for scholarly communication on all aspects of theory, design, and research bearing on the use of simulations of social processes. Contributors to the journal include sociologists, political scientists, economists, psychologists, and educators.

Group and Organization Studies. Published by University Associates, Inc. (7596 Eads Avenue, La Jolla, California 92037).

This quarterly journal is designed to bridge the gap between research and practice for group facilitators involved in the broad field of human relations training. Types of articles include data-based research articles, research and evaluation paradigms, action research, case studies, and critiques of research. There is an emphasis on cross-cultural applications.

BOOKS

Blake, R.R., and J.S. Mouton. *Making Experience Work: The Grid Approach to Critique.* New York: McGraw-Hill, 1978.

Keeton, M. *Experiential Learning: Rationale, Characteristics, and Assessment.* San Francisco: Jossey-Bass, 1976.

Pfeiffer, J.W., and J.E. Jones. *The Annual Handbook for Group Facilitators.* La Jolla, California: University Associates, 1972, 1973, 1974, 1975, 1976, 1977, 1978, and 1979.

Pfeiffer, J.W., and J.E. Jones. *A Handbook of Structured Experiences for Human Relations Training.* (Vols. I-VII.) La Jolla, California: University Associates, 1979.

SIVASAILAM ("THIAGI") THIAGARAJAN is a free-lance trainer, instructional developer, and performance technologist. He is currently working in Gbarnga, Liberia, providing technical assistance to the Ministry of Education on improving the efficiency of elementary school instruction through the application of programmed teaching and learning technologies. Thiagi began his career in education in Madras, India, where he taught high school physics and math for six years. His home-grown instructional innovations attracted the attention of Dr. Douglas Ellson, who invited him to work on a project at Indiana University. Thiagi received his Ph.D in Instructional Systems Technology from Indiana University. His professional experiences in the United States include administering six major instructional development projects, consulting with 40 organizations, and conducting more than 100 workshops all over the country. Thiagi has been the president of the National Society for Performance and Instruction (NSPI) and the Association for Special Education Technology (ASET). He is a prolific writer and has published 12 books, more than 100 articles, 30 audio-visual training packages, and 15 simulations/games. He has been the editor of three professional journals and served on the editorial board of four others.